EAR

EARTHTALES

STORYTELLING IN TIMES OF CHANGE

Alida Gersie

Illustrated by
Ann Winn

First published in 1992 by
Green Print
an imprint of The Merlin Press
10 Malden Road, London NW5 3HR

ISBN 1 85425 065 5

Phototypeset by Computerset Ltd., Harmondsworth, Middlesex
Printed in England by Biddles Ltd., Guildford, Surrey
on recycled paper

398·24

For Thérèse and Antoine

CONTENTS

PART II THE STORIES

To internalise ways of approaching difficulties. The closing stages of a group. Supporting the dream. Strengthened coping with resistance. Stronger visions, longer breaths. Learning to complete. To go our very own way. And still, we celebrate.

Working with the stories

PART III THE STORY FORETOLD

Do you remember? Well, I never forgot. Telling and re-telling and telling again. The continuing thread of wonder. Some closing comments. That this may be, I add to your breath now. . . .

INTRODUCTION

Storytelling is currently experiencing a considerable revival of interest. This has led many educators and people who work in community development to think about ways in which storytelling can be used to explore important shared themes and visions, using ancient folktales and myths to enable people from different cultures and backgrounds to reach out towards one another.

The current concern about environmental issues is connected with this revival, since folktales about the relationship between the earth and its human inhabitants have been at the heart of storytelling since earliest times. Not only do such stories offer a source of inspiration, they also contain a potential for understanding the many ways in which we value and devalue our beautiful green and blue planet, whilst the tales also provide us with practical insight into approaches to our most pressing environmental difficulties.

Earthtales contains forty-two myths and folktales from many different cultures and tribal peoples. They have been chosen for their engrossing and unforgettable qualities, but above all because each tale is directly pertinent to issues in environmental education and community action.

The stories have been grouped around seven themes, which represent recognisable phases of change in a group. They were carefully selected to match part of the process of greening our collective consciousness.

Every story is accompanied by suggestions for exploring one of the story's central themes in groups or in the classroom. These suggestions include many creative-expressive techniques. The storymaking structures enable the group to work together towards solutions, and above all to enhance the group's sense of self-worth and self-determination.

Although *Earthtales* is designed as a practical handbook to contribute to the bringing about of change, the stories themselves – which make up the bulk of the book – can be read in their own right, thus providing a unique collection of ancient stories about the earth and our relationship with the sources of our wellbeing and nourishment.

THREE VIGNETTES FROM PRACTICE

But the dreams their children dreamed
Fleeting, unsubstantial, vain
Shadowy as the shadows seemed,
Airy nothing, as they deemed,
These remain.
MARY COLERIDGE

One

She was an eight-year-old girl, who lived in a flat on the tough housing estate where I worked. Her face showed a perpetual frown. The daily after-school care for her two younger brothers was getting her down. That day she came to the centre, face badly scratched, knees bleeding. Young Thomas clung to her skirt. He wailed. In between sobs Mary scowled her way through the story of bullying children who had said bad things about her mother, her little brothers and above all herself. Being one who did not take insults lightly, she had risen to the occasion, trying to fight her way towards dignity. She had lost. As far as she was concerned, on all scores. Humiliation and revenge were all that remained. After she had dressed her wounds a little, we sat and talked and drank a cup of tea. As Mary liked stories, I asked her after a while if she wanted to hear one. She nodded in troubled consent. I decided to tell her an ancient Bushman myth. This is the story.

It happened a long time ago. In those days the animals lived in huts and cooked their food in pots over a fire. They were animal-people. In a field near their village lived a ghastly monster. From his mouth dribbled a thick layer of green slime. His name was Foulmouth, the Ogre. If you had the courage to look carefully at him you saw how, inside his mouth dark, rotting teeth were covered in hairy mould. He had two long paws with fierce, curled nails at the end of spiky bones. He was gruesome to behold.

Grandmother Blue Crane was one of the animal people. She liked going out into the field with the young animal-girls, trying to look after them. This wasn't always easy for the girls were very lively and she was very old. One day they had as usual gone out into the fields. Some of the girls were playing, others had a rest and one or two were digging for food. Grandmother Blue Crane quietly sat in the grass, when suddenly she called out: 'Go home. Hurry home everyone.' The girls just laughed and made fun of her. But she more strongly urged them to move. 'Go . . . go . . . ,' she shouted. They wondered why old Grandmother Blue Crane was making such a fuss. Then one of the girls looked round. She screamed and started to run. Others looked too and rushed away as fast as their legs would go. They had seen Foulmouth, the Ogre. Grandmother Blue Crane again shouted: 'Hurry. Hurry everyone,' and then: 'Oh . . . Tortoise-girl.' Slow, slow Tortoise-girl was struggling to escape. But the girl's legs didn't carry her fast enough. Again Blue Crane called: 'Hurry, my child. Hurry.' Foulmouth was getting closer and closer. Then Grandmother Blue Crane turned around to face him. 'Leave her alone,' she begged. 'Don't attack the slow one. Fight with me.' Foulmouth just growled and tried to push her out of his way. 'Not the young one. Auck. Leave her alone.' Again he dragged her aside. But she clung to him, urging Tortoise-girl to run, run. Again Foulmouth struck Grandmother Blue Crane for he knew that once they reached the village all would be lost. Then he would have to retreat. His prey would have escaped him. 'Oh Tortoise-girl . . . hurry,' Grandmother's voice was weakening. Foulmouth hit her once more and swung himself towards Tortoise-girl. But it was too late. Tortoise-girl had reached the edge of the fields. With one final sweep Foulmouth pushed Grandmother Blue Crane onto Tortoise-girl's back. Then he disappeared. Gentle Tortoise-girl carried Grandmother Blue Crane to her own home. The village-people rushed towards them. They looked after Grandmother Blue Crane until she was well again. They honoured her.

Mary sighed, stood up and said: 'I'll go and play now.' She left our office holding her head just a little higher. A few minutes later she stuck her face round the door again. 'Those kids have come in. Could you have a word?' We found a space and sat down. Mary, the other children and myself. Quite a few things needed to be aired. There were mutual apologies and the bullying stopped. Mary did not speak about Foulmouth and Grandmother Blue Crane for some time. Then all she said was: 'It wasn't good enough that he stayed in the fields, was it?' I wondered what or who she was referring to. 'That Foulmouth, remember?'

Two

'I don't want to talk about being ill. I've come here to enjoy myself.'

The woman looked at me and demonstratively started to put the lids back on to the pots of fingerpaints.

'You just tell us a happy story.' She added: 'I'm warning you. It's got to be a happy story.'

'You're the ones who'll do the storytelling,' I said. 'I'm asking you to imagine newness. To remember paradise. Of all possible places, please, think about the one called paradise. Whatever you imagine it to be.'

Amidst grumbles and declarations of protest, a silence was born, memories of longings and dreams of good times generated images of paradise. Then I asked the group of elderly women, who were users of a day centre for people with physical disabilities, to paint a picture of the smells, the scent of paradise. They looked at me reproachfully. A picture of the scent of paradise? But the lids were once more removed from the pots of fingerpaint and seven people worked with devoted concentration. Before the women finished their work I asked that they have a good look around their paradise and choose something special which gave them delight. Once something had been chosen they made a brief note or a small drawing of this 'something special'.

We then shared the images of this paradisical place.

'It's luscious and sunny,' said Doreen.

'You can just talk with all the animals. They aren't frightened,' Viv added.

Mary described the sound of trickling water and the stunning colours. Heather talked about the fact that whatever you were looking for, you could find it in this place. And everyone agreed that paradise equalled bliss.

This was our second storymaking session in the day centre where I had been asked to run a short-term group for any users who wished to attend. During the first session we had focused on myths of creation, beginnings and the unknown. The group had shared experiences of making something with very few means. There was pride in the sharing of resourcefulness. Today we were visiting paradise. Images had been painted, a special something had been selected, then the next task needed to be engaged with. I suggested that they could write a letter to someone, inviting this person to visit the paradise which had just been imagined. They would really try to write a tempting invitation. I mentioned how in an ancient Celtic story, Midhir, the lord of the fairies, begins his invitation with: 'Fair woman, will you go with me to a wonderful land where music is . . . ?' We talked a little about these words.

The group felt very dubious about this further task, until Doris said: 'We could invite one of us.' It was decided that they would choose the person for whom the invitation was meant once it had been written. They wrote and wrote. Then names were drawn and each woman received a letter inviting her to visit a paradise. Everyone had also invited someone to visit their own newly imagined land.

The letters were read in silence. Several group members appeared quite moved. They said that it would be nice to share the letters by reading them out loud. Heather began. She stopped halfway through the reading and searched for her handkerchief.

'I'm sorry. It is such a wonderful place,' she said.

The words she had read were:

'This is a beautiful place – lots of everything. But without you I'll be lonesome.'

Before the afternoon had finished a great deal of sharing had taken place about the pain of loneliness, about deteriorating health, the lack of felt warmth and about trees which had been felled. They also talked about the continuing awareness of wellbeing even though too much pain tended to push pleasure into the background. It was Dot who reminded us that at the beginning of the session she had said that she didn't want to talk about pain. She added:

'I didn't know that I could talk about what's difficult and still enjoy myself. Look at my picture, everyone.'

In trembling lines she had drawn the image of a young tree in tender, full bloom. She wagged her finger at us:

'Don't you forget it – that's me – underneath it all,' she said.

We continued our journey through themes of birth, death and life for five more sessions. A few months after the final session there was a follow-up meeting. The women said how they had continued with their own stories. They had made some into storybooks illustrated with their own finger-paintings. The books had been presented to the adjacent nursery school. They were also now involved in telling stories next door. They said:

'It's important to tell the children about all they'll lose if they aren't more careful than we were.'

The group had been started to rekindle people's love of life. The emergence of the wish to share their concern and enjoyment in story form with younger generations was a great bonus.

Three

David was a primary schoolteacher in his mid-thirties. He had chosen teaching as a career because he enjoyed the company of children as well as the processes of learning and discovery. Over the years his dreams were tossed about by administrative demands, seemingly endless curriculum changes and reorganisation plans. The children were difficult too, but as he liked teaching *per se*, they were the least of his problems. His disillusionment was such that he was seriously considering a change of career.

Before making up his mind whether or not to hand in his notice, David came to a one-week course in creative groupwork methods. It was the third day of the course. The group had jelled well. We had talked together, laughed and cried. Above all we had worked, practising new movement patterns as well as various ways of entering into dramatic improvisation. We had also made masks and discovered a hundred and one ways of making stories.

Then the group prepared for an improvisation based on a Bushman myth of creation. They planned to use the masks as well as drumming, movement and sound. The myth tells us that:

> In the time before time the earth is covered in water. A
> vast expanse of water. On the water floats a flower. The
> only flower. Bee takes Mantis from endless, endless space.
> He carries Mantis across the water. At last he finds the
> only flower. Bee leaves Mantis on the flower and returns
> to endless space. Mantis is the maker of fire, keeper of the
> dream. On this flower it begins. It all began in the
> dreamtime. In the time before time.

The dramatisation had been so structured that each group member would be given the opportunity to play the roles of Bee, Mantis, the Flower, endless space and the vast expanse of water. It was David's turn to play Mantis. As Mantis he clung to Bee in dogged determination; he struggled not to be left alone on the only flower in a vast universe. He cried into the emptiness. Would nobody hear him? Would nobody come to rescue him? The other performers whispered in urgent chorus: 'Mantis, Keeper of the dream . . . Keeper of the dream?'

Slowly and gradually David as Mantis rose. He danced his own dance of transformation. Moving from abandoned helplessness into potent creator. When his dance was completed he rejoined the drama's pattern. Soon the enactment reached its fulfilment. The performers demasked and the careful process of deroling began, offering the opportunity to recognise aspects of the role as familiar. Other feelings which arose whilst in role, and forms of dramatic expression with which they had felt less identified, could then be surrendered to the timelessness of the performance. When it was David's turn to speak, he looked radiant. He said that he did not yet have words for what had happened. He simply knew that his Mantis dance had not only been a dance of transformation within the context of the drama, something had changed within him. He did not yet know what.

David's real pleasure in what he had discovered during the enactment lasted all week. He spoke a great deal more about work, life and love. When the course finished he returned to his job and soon realised that he needed to change schools rather than give up teaching. Some time later I received a letter in which he talked about the impact of the Mantis dance. It had marked a turning point. He now used many ancient stories in his work to strengthen the children's bond with life and to help them give form to environmental issues. He wrote:

'Once my own bond with creation had been revitalised I knew what I wanted to do and what I could do. It gave me the courage of my own conviction. Thanks.'

PART I
WHEN STORIES ARE TOLD

1 PLEASE TELL ME A STORY

Nothing in the world is single;
All things by a law divine
In one spirit meet and mingle.
Why not I with thine?
PERCY BYSSHE SHELLEY

Suppose it is late afternoon. We are enjoying the company of family or friends. After a while silence falls. A comfortable silence. Then someone asks: 'Will you tell us a story?' We probably feel quite tongue-tied. Wondering how to respond. Our mind has suddenly gone blank. The stories we do remember seem to be either boring, inappropriate or very incomplete. More often than not we hear ourselves say: 'Can't I read you a story, instead?' A pile of books is pulled out. Together we pick up one book, then another, until our young or not-so-young friend stops the picking and choosing, saying: 'This one.' Storytime begins. The listener settles down and relaxes into hearing new or familiar words, spoken by someone who cares enough to take some time and read a tale.

Later we may find fragments of half-forgotten narratives playing through our mind. Incomplete stories linger promisingly, as if prodding us into retelling. But we did not give them enough time to become whole again, to be reconstructed out of memory and fantasy. We may wonder a while how exactly the story went or why we were so reluctant to tell our own tale, and then continue with the business of the day or night.

In Korea the following tale was told to address the consequences of our inability to tell the tales which come our way, the reluctance to speak the story of our life.

> A long time ago there lived a boy whose parents died
> when he was very young. Now he shared the house with
> an old uncle. Every night before this boy went to sleep, his
> uncle told him a story. The boy loved these stories. They
> were magnificent. The other children in the village knew
> that the old man was a great storyteller and they often
> begged the boy to share the tales which his uncle had told
> him. He invariably refused.
>
> In a corner of the boy's bedroom hung a wonderful,
> old leather bag. This bag was tightly closed with a piece
> of string. No one ever paid much attention to the bag. It
> seemed as if it had always been there. But whenever the
> uncle told a story, the bag would open just a little and the

story-spirit disappeared into it. It had nowhere else to go until the boy would tell the story again. Then the story-spirit could be released from the bag. But as you know, the boy refused to tell the stories. Not even one. Therefore the bag became more and more crowded. Cramped and struggling with each other for space, the story-spirits were very miserable.

When the boy grew up, a marriage was arranged. The young man had just left the house on the way to the wedding ceremony, when the uncle heard some groaning sounds. They came from his nephew's old bedroom. The man went into the room to see where the wretched moaning noises were coming from.

Suddenly he saw the swirling of the old leather bag. As if something inside wanted to get out. The man kept very quiet. He heard the story-spirits speak. They were planning revenge. The boy had left them there hanging in the corner of his bedroom. Something had to be done. Because they had been marvellous stories full of danger and adventure, they thought of some very evil acts.

One was going to poison the young bridegroom, another would burn him and a third would turn into a

snake, hide near the bridal bed and kill him. This story
laughed an evil laugh. The other story-spirits cheered.

The uncle was horrified. He had loved the boy all his
life, even though he had wondered why he would never
tell a story. He wanted to protect him now that he knew
the stories' plans.

The couple's wedding-day was very peculiar, full of
adventure and mis-adventure. They wondered what the
old man was up to. All day long he appeared in the
strangest places, behaving most oddly. But the limit was
reached when they had just retired to their bedroom. In
rushed the old man, sword drawn, a lamp in his hand.
Ignoring their angry reproaches he searched the room.
Near the boy's pillow was a giant snake ready to pounce.
The old man killed the snake. Having heard the great
commotion in the bridal bedroom, other guests hurried to
the room. They demanded to know what had happened.
Then the old man told the tale of the trapped story-spirits
and their planned revenge. The young couple understood
that he had saved their life. The bridegroom spoke,
saying: 'It need not have been this way. I promise to tell
and retell the stories that have come my way. I promise I
will.' The story-spirits were well satisfied. The next day
the newly wed couple collected the leather bag from the
uncle's house. It stayed near the young man wherever he
went, and whenever anyone asked, he told them a story,
even if only a little one.

This is how one of Korea's greatest storytellers came to
be.

We all have our own storybag filled with memories, events and the
stories we ourselves were once told. The calamities which may befall us
when we don't tell our tales may not be quite so vividly dramatic as the
ones which befell the young bridegroom on his wedding day, though
there is a price which all of us pay when stories are withheld. We are
deprived from gaining direct and intimate knowledge of collective
experiences. Whenever stories are absent from our social interactions
this results in a decreased sense of community; the absence even of a
sense of belonging. The crucial interpersonal space in which we can
identify to our heart's delight is then lost. It becomes more difficult to
try out possibilities in the imagination.

More dangerously, the withholding of stories adds to taboos, secrecy
and to the fear that misfortune singles people out. People who are then

required not to break the silence. The reluctance to tell our tales also means that we miss out on the more subtle and playful opportunities for communication. When asking to hear a story, chances are that our listeners would settle for more or less any story, provided we were true to its content and honest in our desire to share this tale now in this place.

Occasionally most of us feel alone and somewhat bare. Then we need companionship to soothe the clefts which have emerged within us. A little bit of lifting beyond our preoccupation with ourselves will not do us any harm. In fact, it is likely to do us some good. Whenever we request a story we do so trusting that a web of possibility can be woven between ourselves and the other person. A web which contains our awareness of alternatives and which reflects the bond which we have with one another. Our commitment too to life. It has been said that 'the challenge of today is to save the planet from further devastation which violates both the enlightened self-interest of humans and non-humans and decreases the potential of joyful existence for all.'

The maintenance of this joy is the implicit function of storytelling. The clarification of 'enlightened self-interest' is frequently its purpose. Whereas the prevention of such violation is invariably at the heart of ancient tales.

2 ON STORIES AND STORYTELLING

Now sleeps the crimson petal, now the white;
Nor waves the cypress in the palace walk;
Nor wakes the gold fin in the porphyry font;
The fire-fly wakens: waken thou with me.
ALFRED LORD TENNYSON

Stories alert us to the possibility of betterment. Not necessarily because they have happy endings. Old folktales often don't. But because a story evokes in the listener an 'if only' response, jolting us into the awareness that life could be different, both for better and for worse. We are reminded of alternatives. Our attention is directed towards the unexplained and the unexpected. In stories a known situation functions as the starting point for an exploration of the not-yet-known, that which surprises and maybe frightens us. Through listening to the ancient tales we are offered increased knowledge of various ways to approach the unfamiliar. What we do with this knowledge is for us to decide. The tales simply convey that fact and fiction are close relatives. Once the previously unnamed is named, the alien object or the unusual experi-ence has received communicable form. Thereby such experiences become identifiable and recognisable. The old story will survive until it evokes more questions than it answers. Then an altogether new tale is created to contain our concern and to enhance our curiosity.

We listen to stories not just because we need companionship or want to be entertained. When our life is complex, which it is more often than not, we hope to find within the story images relevant to our own predicament, hoping, maybe against hope, that an answer to our problem might dwell *within* the story, not yet realising that the solution often emerges from our heartfelt response *to* the tale. In times of serious trouble we need someone who will pay attention to our predicament, who will help us to find a different perspective or simply share our worries. Then we must communicate our experience. Communication which relies on sounds, gestures, images and words; combined, these contribute to the story of our life. However, the difficulty is that when we are troubled, we are often also confused, quite unable to make sense of our situation. Events may have caused us such pain that it feels impossible to express what has happened. Matters are sometimes also compounded by feelings of shame or guilt. Our ability to articulate the unmentionable is then grievously curtailed. When this is the case stories may help for they offer us a language to describe the occurrences and through which we can highlight our predicament. Let us therefore consider some other important facets of stories and storytelling.

Please, imagine a small village on a remote island. It is the time of twilight. Old people can be seen to wander towards the village meeting place: a few wooden benches beneath the trees. They sit down in what seem to be their customary places, overlooking a valley. The odd word breaks the day's silence. Then one of the people, face wrinkled, hands sparkling with softness and experience, begins to tell a tale. Weariness drops away. The others enter into the never-never land of ancient time and space. Accompanying the storyteller into a different world where the deliberations of rabbits, foxes and a girl's courage are all that matter.

The dimensions of such tales are cosmic. The main character, the protagonist, whether mouse or king moves from the known environment to a less familiar world, from culture into nature, from the tame to the wild. We identify with such story-journeys because the pattern of separation, initiation and return is characteristic of many of our own processes of development. Most paths of story-adventure are a magnification of aspects of our journey through life. In order to mature each of us needs to let go of old ideas and habits. Discover alternative ways of being and then to integrate the new and the old, so that we may achieve true maturation. To develop informed concern.

To facilitate this process of maturation myths and folktales have been told from one generation to another since time immemorial. Some of these stories were written down. Others were simply told and retold, becoming part of the oral history of a people. Whenever a storyteller shared such an old tale faithfulness to the received story mattered. After all every ancient story bears witness to the distilled wisdom of many generations. In most communities, the story-guardians consequently carried special responsibilities. The Ekoi people of Nigeria characterised the tasks of the storyteller as follows:

> He or she needed to honour each story-child's wonderful gown. This outfit had to be special yet clearly related to the gowns of all other story-children.

> Secondly the storyteller had to remember that every story-child is nourished by what is hidden as well as by the embrace of both rich and poor, day and night.

> Thirdly the storyteller had to accept the story-child's need for veracity and authenticity. Its own truth must be spoken. It demands no more but also no less.

> Finally the storyteller needed to let the story-child run free. This could happen in one way only. The story had to be given voice. For thereby the story-child was given birth and received life anew. Thus it could remain, perhaps forever, on earth.

Any tale told is like a remembered adventure. Through the act of telling we allow someone else access to our experiences, to our inner world and the wisdom or folly we have gained. Once the story has been set free, the tale begins a life of its own, independent of the teller. From then on both the listener and the teller decide what will next happen to the tale. It becomes vulnerable to alteration and change. A potentially wayward story-child. Even though the tale may be repeated, it will never be quite the same again. In that sense each story is told only once. 'In this time . . . in this place . . . for me . . . for you . . . because of what is happening here and now. Thus it is always old and ever new; the same and yet continuously different.'

As said before we listen to a story amongst others because we are in search of information. The gift of curiosity inspires our need to inquire and to discuss what we have found. However, we may also use such apparent activity in order to be distracted, to prevent action from occurring. In spite of a seeming quest for understanding, many of us hold back on the threshold of change, casting a veil of forgetfulness over what we know to be true. This happens when the newly discovered perspectives hurt too much. The pain thus caused leads to a felt sense of being overwhelmed and unable to cope. We are then tempted to lull ourselves into a depressed sense of security, which is supported by the all too fragile belief that somehow things will be righted, even though we refrain from action.

The ancient storytellers were well aware of our contradictory human propensities. They therefore told stories both to strengthen the motivation to persevere with processes of innovation and to slow down hasty attempts at implementing change. At times the apparent maintenance of the status quo needs to be encouraged, simply to prevent the adoption of premature, ill-considered newness, for this often leads to bitter disappointment and enhances a growing reluctance to try out appropriate innovations at a later stage. However, such slowing down can only be defended if it truly serves the function of strengthening an enduring capacity to bring about effective change.

Nowadays we may chance across storytellers in schools, churches, libraries and community centres. The occasions which call for the telling of an old story are often centred around major events, such as a leaving do, a wedding or a funeral. Others are connected with the time of year, like Christmas or the return of spring. We mark these occasions because the alternation of the seasons calls for adjustment. Our need for a story being intimately linked with major alterations in the circumstances of our life. During such a time of transition we tend to seek the company of people who are important to us, to be reminded of the many ways in which our individual life is embedded within the greater life of the community, beyond the immediacy of the here and now. Stories offer such a link.

When balancing our personal, emotional books we may be tempted to neglect the little, nameless acts of kindness and of love. Yet we need to acknowledge such acts because they nourish our faith in benignity and truthfulness. Consequently most healthy communities also arrange to meet once in a while to highlight the connections between the individual deeds or omissions and collective wellbeing. So that the place which we may have grown used to describing as bleak without and bare within, can be honoured once more with appreciative eyes. At the start of such a gathering the participants may well have felt utterly poor in the poor place. Thanks to the listening to one another's tales, those present leave inspired by a renewed sense of belonging, with a clearer commitment to make the dreams of betterment come true.

3 STORYMAKING IN GROUPS

Repeat that, repeat
Cuckoo, bird, and open ear wells
heart-springs delightfully sweet
with a ballad, with a ballad, a rebound
GERARD MANLEY HOPKINS

Most of us are familiar with 'doing drama' with a group of people or with making music together. Once in a while we may dance or play games with others in a more or less organised way. Storymaking is a mixture of all of these activities, whilst additionally, during the session, a personal story is created. This story is closely related to a folktale or myth, which is shared with the group.

I would like you to accept the premise that every one of us has the capacity to tell a tale. It may be very short such as the first tale an unhappy young man told during a storymaking workshop: 'The traveller came to the sea and saw the dead pigeon. It had been washed ashore.' When asked to explore what happened next, he immediately closed up and said: 'Nothing. How would I know?' The group persisted, saying that of course he knew a great deal more about that little story. He muttered that he would tell us later. The 'later' tale arrived:-

> He told the group about the pigeon's illness. How
> lonesome it had been. Then – one day – the pigeon gave
> up. It died. Now it was just lying there on the beach. The
> traveller, who had come to the beach, saw the pigeon. It
> made him think of his father's death. He hadn't been able
> to attend the funeral. He was a wanderer. He sat by the
> pigeon for a little while. Then he lifted it up and carried it
> way beyond the reach of the sea. He buried the pigeon. He
> didn't mark the grave. But he buried the little bird. Then
> the traveller decided that he would go back to visit his
> home village. He went on his way.

After having listened to the story the group members took a small piece of paper in order to paint or write a small gift for the traveller who decided to return to his home village maybe for a fleeting visit, maybe to stay for a while. The gifts were handed to the young man, who was somewhat surprised and embarrassed by the sudden abundance of 'goodies'. 'It's like Christmas,' he said. He looked at his gifts and was visibly touched by several of them. Then he selected a couple which he was particularly pleased to accept on behalf of the traveller in his story. These were the two gifts:

A bag filled with little presents to share with the children in the traveller's home village;
An old locket with a photo of the traveller's father as a young man.

He looked around the circle and said to everyone. 'Thanks for all the presents. You know I've got no family. I haven't had presents for years. Haven't had any dough to buy any either. I didn't know you could make such lovely presents. Thanks ever so much.'

He was moved. All of us were moved. Then we listened to another story and made more gifts.

During a storymaking session group members are encouraged to give both voice and image to their knowledge and experience of life in story form. The extent to which the happenings in these stories are consciously connected with real life events or real life fantasies depends on the group facilitator, the group members and the purpose of the storymaking work.

If we accept that each story is a journey, then we can say that the act of embarking on a storymaking journey affirms us as people who can travel, which tells us that:

we are strong and well enough to be able to leave base;
we are sufficiently motivated to undertake something;
we have inner resources to overcome anticipated difficulties;
we are some-one; namely the one who goes on a journey.

In the process of creating a story we both require and acquire:

an awareness of I and other;
an awareness of time: past, present and future;
an awareness of place: here as well as there;
an awareness of sequentiality, causality, the accidental, the unexpected and the anticipated, the predictable and the unpredictable;
an awareness of boundaries (beginning, middle and end);
an awareness of order and chaos, the known and the unknown.

In a storymaking group we work with the exploration of inner-outer world connections and with the relevance of the metaphors thus generated to our lives. The work is based on the assumption that all our

stories or metaphoric utterances are a representation of our interpretation of reality. They are the result of the process of confrontation and
interaction between our inner and outer world.

During a series of sessions a group meets to explore a shared theme of
concern. Such themes may be 'environmental troubles', 'the felt sense of
a loss of direction', or 'the need to find support'. Each workshop lasts
approximately an hour and a half. During this time the group members
paint, write, move, act, talk. Things they have mostly never done before
and would probably regard as either silly, kids' work, or irrelevant. An
additional early barrier to storymaking work is formed by the sense
which many people have that they could never do or say anything
original or interesting. Let alone something which they might call
'artistic'. Every exercise in this book, as well as the sequence of the tasks,
is therefore designed to diminish performance anxiety, and to ease the
participants, almost surreptitiously, into unselfconscious enjoyment of
symbolic expression.

The self-authored stories are generated in various ways as is revealed
by a quick glance through the storymaking structures which accom-
pany the folktales and myths. These self-generated stories are always
closely related to the story outline contained in the ancient tale. The
personal, contemporary tale is thus based on the underlying structure of
the old story, which has – as it were – the personal tale superimposed
upon its ancient base. When the new stories are read, the listeners (the
other group members) are asked to undertake a specific task as soon as
they have finished listening to the story. These response tasks have a
number of purposes:

they help the listener to listen, enhancing listening skills;

they help the listener to respond concisely, facilitating a wide range
of communication skills;

they enable people to give form to feelings, expanding our
symbolic/expressive range;

they provide evidence to the storyteller, that she/he has been heard
and often understood. This reassures us and builds trust between
people.

After a period of reflection, the session is closed. The participants return
to their various homes, whatever these may be: a prison-cell or a villa,
hostel accommodation or a children's home, a flat on a housing estate or
a hospital ward. People who participate in these sessions have come
from all walks of life with widely differing complexities which they have
to endure or resolve. Some have become the reluctant prisoners of high-
powered jobs, others are prisoners of their inability to contain impulses.
Many are children attending school. Some are men and women who,

finding life too confusing, embraced drink, drugs or depression. Others are fighting terminal illness or run voluntary organisations. So many reasons why we join a group of people to make a few stories. So many reasons, too, why we may wish to acquire the skills of storymaking. Maybe in order to nurture the quality of communication in our groups at work. Maybe to facilitate different ways of meeting in the voluntary organisations to which we belong. When people leave the session they may take with them a story which they created as well as numerous gifts. The story is theirs, a witness to their life, a container of possibility. The gifts are also theirs, evidence of real links with other people. Though still alone, for we cannot make one another unalone, the 'gifts' contribute to a renewed sense of belonging. During the workshops voice has been given to strengths, to ways of coping and to ways of not being able to cope at all. Because this happens in the presence of others, the participants glimpse and simultaneously experience the reality of possible change.

But let us return to the discussion of the key components of a storymaking session. As said, in the storymaking workshops the group members are introduced to an ancient tale which they will probably be able to retell many years later. This is paradoxically easier if the tale is unfamiliar. Such a 'foundation' story is chosen because it is relevant to this group at that time. The selection is based on one of the following criteria:

   the story is pertinent to an issue which interests the group;

   it reflects the process and dynamics of the group;

   it addresses a preoccupation of one or several group members;

   it offers alternative approaches to experienced difficulties.

The stories chosen for the workshops have primarily been created by people or tribes whose way of life is severely threatened, or has already been destroyed. Group members frequently express wonder and awe at the beauty of an Inuit (Eskimo), Bushman, Cheyenne or Maori tale. Because each tale bears witness to the profound knowledge and wisdom of the people who gave it birth, the telling of such a story can also contribute to the raising of our awareness with regard to our prejudices. So much the better if the story becomes a bridge across which people from different places, in different times and with other predicaments, can meet to address their shared longing for a good enough life.

The old story is then used in conjunction with a storymaking structure which can also be called a story-pattern. The group members are invited to participate in a journey through this structure. As noted the group members thereby engage in a wide range of creative-expressive tasks or exercises. The purpose of these exercises may at times seem obscure. Yet the tasks have been carefully designed and sequenced in order to encourage:

the group members' confidence in their creative-expressive abilities;

the steady development of spontaneity (whilst circumventing the 'be spontaneous' paradox);

a group culture in which mutual support flourishes;

the dimution of anxiety, to build confidence and to stimulate tolerance of difference and ambiguity, so that learning and change can happen.

Through participation in storymaking the group members hopefully gain the following:

familiarisation with a folktale or myth;

a self-authored story which is linked with the ancient tale;

the experience of working together with other people in a way which is exploratory and stimulating;

the experience of being heard and responded to;

a few paintings, sculptures and other people's written or painted gifts.

In my experience group members frequently say that the journey around the ancient story has been re-vitalising, thought-provoking or oddly comforting. This is probably achieved because storymaking is both a recreation and a form of community therapy, working on many levels from the private to the public, the hidden to the shared. Most of all participants are helped to contact their creative energy. The work involves the development of listening skills, memory and the evocation of creative responses. Group members quickly lose their inhibitions about trying out ideas. They grow to enjoy themselves. Surprise and wonder at the richness of our inner worlds is often voiced. This experience is of course in itself deeply satisfying. Because so much of the work is focused around giving and receiving, it also becomes possible to explore material of substantial inner significance without the arousal of too high a level of anxiety. This in turn contributes to the early development of group cohesion and intimacy. Group morale is thereby heightened. This matters especially when the workshops take place in a school or an institution.

Above all the old and the new stories paraphrase our fears, giving form to our ability to act constructively in the face of such predicaments. Thereby we grow stronger, amongst other reasons because we realise that we can be loved as well as liked even though there is a great deal we urgently need to learn. That's something. It is quite a lot when we face the fact that we must change our way of being, because our current way of being is badly attacking the earth on which we live and depend.

4 ISSUES OF ENVIRONMENTAL CONCERN

. . . then the wolf rages wild,
And the lion glares thro' the dun forest:
The fleeces of our flocks are cover'd with
Thy sacred dew; protect them with thine influence.
WILLIAM BLAKE

Storymaking is based on the assumption that we are not free to say we see not, nor is genuine concern for the threats which are posed to the future of life on earth optional. We can of course wish that hope, love and the desire for constructive action will be miraculously bestowed upon us. We can also take care to generate these within ourselves. We know that:

hope is what we do with our despair;

love is what we do with our bitterness;

faith is what we do with our disbelief.

Such doing makes sense. Even though it may sometimes be necessary to adopt a 'wait and see' approach, many a time we wait to the detriment of our capacity to act constructively and protectively. Until our will atrophies due to a lack of exercise, or a belated awareness that we ought to have done something, didn't and are now paralysed by guilt. All of us know that the sparkling dew drops do not stay and that we ourselves will surely die. However, we frequently prefer to embrace a life of 'let's pretend that it is not happening', because the full measure of such knowing is too unsettling. We are so often afraid to let go and frightened of change. Whenever our reality feels too painful the pull towards denial and sleepy indolence is great. In relation to environmental issues it is profoundly disquieting that:

if the current trend continues one species in three or five could be extinct by the middle of the next century; then there may be little else left to protect but cows and sugar cane;

in many cases the wild is already little more than a mega-zoo;

in every country land is overcultivated, overgrazed, cleared of vegetation and inappropriately irrigated.

yet more than 40,000 children die every day of malnutrition.

whilst recovery and rest have frequently been replaced by exhaustion and burn-out both in terms of land-use and our own patterns of activity.

meanwhile we ignore that more than £1 million per minute is spent on armaments.

Most of us want to call a halt to starvation, poverty and to the irreversible and cumulative processes of destruction and species elimination which occur hour upon hour. We try to be fully aware that we cannot have the species of plants, insects and animals which we removed today from the earth's surface, back tomorrow. Earth is not a playpen inhabited by a screaming toddler who demands care and attention by throwing the toys out of the playpen in the hope that a caring adult will sooner or later return them. When species disappear they are irrevocably lost. But what does irrevocable loss mean in factual and above all in emotional terms? We have difficulties talking about the death of people who matter to us. Oftentimes we find it impossible to mourn. How can we then be expected to mourn the extinction of the sabre-toothed tiger, the woolly rhino and the giant ground sloth? Given that we already have such trouble with the intimate events of our own life, how can we even begin to prepare for the imminent disappearance of the giant panda, the echo parakeet and the humpback whale? Let alone the other:

555 species of mammals
1073 species of birds
186 species of reptiles
54 species of amphibians
596 species of fishes
2125 species of invertebrates.

All of whom are in immediate danger of extinction. In our mind's eye we support the suggestion that workable solutions to many of the problems which we have created for the earth must urgently be found: solutions which will often combine traditional techniques with new ideas. We too want the trap of self-generating and self-sustaining poverty to be overcome, preferring to think of ourselves as people of good will, who happen to get caught in intergroup processes where each side tends to exaggerate its own virtues as well as the other side's capacity for destructive action. Repeatedly there are good grounds for feeling that we are simply at the mercy of powerful people who seem to be reluctant to own up to their mistakes and errors. Realising belatedly that such power-figures offer us the opportunity to point our finger and attribute blame, whilst at the same time giving us an excuse to do little as regards the bringing about of those changes which are well within our reach. For however appropriate our accusations may be, we also recognise that the attribution of responsibility and blame to forces beyond our apparent control tends to limit our desire for constructive action. It restricts our horizon and thereby undermines our determination to bring about change. We need to free ourselves from the entrancement with the exclusive attribution of external cause and effect, and wake up to the full realisation that there are many things which we can do to express our reverence for life, which includes all people, animals and nature. The interests of future generations matter. We ourselves matter. In spite of an often felt sense of impotence and powerlessness, we do have a profound and lasting effect on the world.

As many of the folktales and myths in this book illustrate, these seeming contradictions dwell at the heart of both the storytelling and the storymaking process.

Due to the specific nature of storymaking the focus of the work stays firmly with the impact we can have on each other, the consequences of our choices and with practising the numerous ways in which we can offer each other support to change in the direction of mutual co-operation and generous initiative-taking. Alternative forms of behaviour aren't just talked about, they are almost imperceptibly rehearsed as an essential part of the process. The consequent change is therefore felt to be natural. It is, because it is the logical result of 'doing' as well as being together in the presence of the distilled wisdom of generations of people. As such the mode of work itself generates vitality, an effect which has been known and therefore consciously used since time immemorial.

The storymaking sessions are so structured that in the course of a series the individual and the group are also enabled:

to work through felt powerlessness and the identification with helplessness or passivity;

to explore various motivations for change as well as implicit or explicit resistance forces;

to discover experientially how stress tends to influence decision-making processes, which are then guided primarily by emotions whilst 'reason' is ignored. This in turn leads to reduced influence and efficacy.

Influence and efficacy are vitally important, especially when the actual survival of people, animals, plants, air and water are at stake.

5 WHEN LIVING THROUGH A TIME OF CRISIS

Shut not so soon; the full-eyed night
Has not as yet begun
To make a seizure on the light,
Or to seal up the sun.
ROBERT HERRICK

In times of crisis we are generally blind to everything outside our immediate necessities. How could we be otherwise? Our survival is at stake and by limiting our field of attention we might indeed weather the storm. The problem with our current environmental crisis is firstly that it does not yet look like much of a crisis, at least not like the ones we have learnt to recognise as such; and secondly that we have to rethink what we consider our basic necessities to be. The bringing about of change in this particular situation is therefore infinitely complex. We are unable to see clearly on several levels and in several ways. As stated earlier, in a crisis we are blind to everything outside our immediate necessities. Yet it is important not to forget that:

what we believe to be basic necessities are contributing to the acceleration of the current crisis;

therefore, in order to resolve the crisis, we must adjust these very same basic necessities;

but in a crisis we cling stubbornly to known satisfactions for that is how we learned to survive, etc. etc.

A destructive double-bind, if ever there was one.

Presently the daily life of a majority of people in the north-western hemisphere is quite comfortable. Though most people may be living comfortably, hedgerows, rivers, dolphins, puffins and the poor and homeless people aren't. If serious notice were to be taken of their plight the environmental crisis would be in the forefront of everyone's mind. We would also realise that every one of us is likely to be affected by the magnitude of the environmental problems before too long, irrespective of status and capabilities. Each living creature or plant will sooner rather than later face substantial difficulties with:

the selection of a habitat which offers 'clean air, clean water and a fertile soil';

comfortable access to abundant food and heat;

protection from threats by others who are competing for increasingly scarce resources.

The trouble is, 'Before how long?' The answer is unclear. Some experts give us ten more years to cling to existing satisfactions, others thirty years or even a little longer. Most specialists, however, agree that if current trends continue unchanged, there is no doubt that one day we shall rudely awaken to the fact that immediate and very drastic action will be required to safeguard even our most basic needs such as clean air and clean water. But because we believe that this day hasn't arrived yet, we are unable to act collectively and constructively to prevent the present situation from worsening, for such are the dynamics of change on a large scale. Unless of course we achieve a dramatic turnabout in human ways of thinking and responding. Then we might learn to prefer prevention over cure. However, until such a turnabout happens we are likely to use one of three major mechanisms to fight off the emergence of anxiety which results from the demand to change – a demand which is

mostly perceived as arising outside of us, instead of internally. To deal
with the 'apparent' scare-mongering of environmentalists and concerned scientists we tend to adopt the following mechanisms:

> We cope with the aroused anxiety by refusing to believe, even in
> the face of overwhelming evidence, that the situation is as bad as
> people say it is. Our old satisfactions cannot be given up without a
> struggle.

> We criticise others, preferably institutions and people in a position
> of power or responsibility, for not doing enough now, or for not
> having done enough earlier. The 'they ought to do/have done
> something' syndrome. This protects us for a while from having to
> take responsibility ourselves.

> We pronounce unequivocally that somehow someone (always
> someone *else*!) will generate a saving idea or even a person. This
> idea or this person will then rescue the situation from the brink of
> disaster.

We are likely to hold on to these three forms of denial until our anxiety,
fear and guilt have been reduced to tolerable levels or until the anticipated calamity is such that we have to act. Meanwhile we listen to voices
like Chris Colwell's, who writes: 'Institutions alone can never solve the
problems that cumulate from the seemingly inconsequential actions of
millions of individuals . . . As much as we are the root of the problem,
we are also the genesis of its solution. Go to it.' If we take his advice and
'go to it' we accept that we can help ourselves and others by strengthening our coping and change-ability skills. In order to do this we need to
set times aside during which:

> discussion of our personal experiences is stimulated;

> the imagination is exercised both as a means to gain self-awareness
> and to nourish wish-fulfilment;

> we experience situations which lead to effective approaches to
> problem-solving and to the resolution of intra-psychic conflict.

Then we soon discover that:

> effective action belongs to the realm of the possible and not to the
> realm of the merely imagined;

> it is in our interest (if nothing else) to learn to refrain from
> devouring or immobilising our little helpmates;

> we must share and co-operate in order to reduce conflict and
> competition over resources.

Why then do ancient stories matter in this process and how do they contribute to bringing about change?

Whenever we listen to a story a special thread of intimacy is created between us, the listeners, and the storyteller. Once the story has captivated our interest, we become enfolded in a private world. The quality of concentration is such that all around are influenced by the prevailing sense of hushedness. We do not wish to disturb the image of completeness evoked by a storyteller and group of listeners temporarily engrossed in an alternative world.

The ebb and flow of the listeners' concentration affect the storyteller. Thereby the listeners become inextricably caught up in the story-web. Through listening we have indicated that we are willing to make space for another life-experience. We permit access to the outside, allowing it to become part of us. New insights and concepts may well be introduced which can be intimidating. We surrender by degrees to the unknown inherent in each tale and trust the guide to know the way. Have you ever wondered why so many children want to hear a story at bedtime or why so many adults read before going to sleep? I suggest that, apart from wishing to delay the moment of embracing unknown dreams and nightmares and therefore clinging to the known of consciousness, we want to hear a story because it performs the function of reassuring us that the unknown can become knowable, that the road between the familiar and the unfamiliar can be travelled both ways. Thus more often than not, stories are told in times of crisis and transition in order to provide reassurance and thereby to strengthen the motivation to change. Traditionally myths and folktales serve a number of functions:

They safeguard and codify information as well as beliefs.

They remind us of other times and different places and lift us beyond our limiting preoccupation with the 'here and now'. Thereby they facilitate the emergence of a fresh perspective on our actual situation. Though inspired *by* the story such a new perspective is of course not a reflection *of* the story.

Stories provide us with a known completion, a unity of form. Each story has a beginning, a middle and an end. Embedded within this structure are a specific conflict and patterns of conflict resolution. These stimulate the development of possible solutions to our own predicaments.

Stories evoke powerful emotional responses. These emotions help us to clarify the way we feel and fuel the desire for change.

They nearly always generate communication. Not only does the listening to a story create a warm bond between us. Once the story is finished we often automatically turn to each other to talk and to share our responses. Likewise a good story invariably evokes the longing to retell it to others.

All of us tell stories to some extent in our daily life. We share memories, gossip or retell events we heard about. Ancient stories differ from these personal tales in so far that they have mattered to people often enough and long enough to acquire a more or less consistent form, which is changed slowly and gradually as the story is adjusted to reflect new strands of distilled wisdom.

When old habits must be changed, because they no longer work, we experience stress. We feel compelled:

to adopt new and more adaptive behaviour patterns;

to modify our roles;

to re-order our expectations.

Such stress can be sharply heightened both by the absence of vital information or by an overload of painful information. The consequent confusion and ambiguity diminish our felt senses of control over our life and behaviour even further. Failure and deterioration are writ large on the anxious screen of our acutely sensitised mind. As Ofra Ayalon, expert on the development of coping strategies in relation to community therapy, warns us, these bring in their wake a parade of old horrors and disappointments.

There is little doubt that a three-pronged approach to dealing with individual and community stress, which is caused by an unavoidable requirement to change, is most effective. This involves:

the working through of earlier traumatic experiences;

the regaining of lost feelings of mastery;

the development of new insights.

Since time immemorial people have used storytelling and story-creation to enhance these processes. It makes sense that in our day and age which saw the rapid demise of storytelling as a public event we now witness a revived interest in this ancient art. Our stresses and serious concerns have suddenly increased a thousand-fold.

6 CONDITIONS FOR CHANGE IN THE GROUP

Weave a bower of love
for birds to meet each other
Weave a canopy above
Nest and egg and mother.
CHRISTINA ROSSETTI

Storymaking works best in groups which formally make use of group-interaction to facilitate change in personal functioning. Such groups can be found in schools and colleges, youth clubs, community and arts centres or adult education institutes. The kind of changes such a storymaking group may hope to achieve amongst its members are:

more willingness to enter into discussion and exchange of ideas;

greater confidence in presenting proposals;

more willingness to take risks;

increased energy levels and greater determination to implement change.

In order to achieve these it would be good if the group could work in a physical environment which is friendly and inviting. A comfortable room with tables to work at and a big enough space for movement or dramatic activities would be useful. So much the better if the room could be free from interruptions, quiet, warm and always available when the group needs it. However, in my experience most rooms which teachers, youth workers and voluntary groups have to use do not meet these basic requirements. I suggest that rather than not run the group, we make do and create as inviting an atmosphere as possible under the circumstances. Two or three interested people soon warm up most spaces, let alone ten or twelve. I have had to work in the old furniture storage area, in concrete cellars without natural light or heating and neglected back rooms of churches with paint peeling off the walls and permeated with the scent of disinfectant. It wasn't easy. Sometimes we had to work hard to generate enthusiasm or some wildness. But it can be done and if that's where we have to start from, so be it.

The teacher or facilitator is often given the initial task of creating and maintaining the group and is therefore expected to make a fundamental contribution to building the group's culture. In my experience these need to be shared with the group at an early stage, so that the group can learn to take responsibility for its own management and functioning.

It may be important to list some of the factors which need to be considered whenever we start a group:

The group's overall objectives have to be clarified. What will be the best approach to achieving those objectives?

Where will the group meet, for how long and how many times? Will the space used be available on all those occasions?

What is the maximum group size? Is everyone expected to attend all the sessions? How is early departure from the group negotiated?

If the group is co-led the facilitators need to set time aside to talk through their approaches, to plan the group together and to reflect on the group at the end of every session.

Who will be the group members? Can anyone join or do we hope to attract/recruit people of a certain age/ability/disposition/with a certain amount of free time? How will we prepare people for the group experience? With the help of a leaflet, a talk or an individual meeting?

How will the boundaries of the group be maintained? What is the shared philosophy which underpins the group's functioning?

Because every group is potentially a powerful instrument to bring about real improvement in our relationships with each other, we need to be aware that 'good' groups are the result of effort and style, rarely of luck. It is possible to foster an exciting group atmosphere in which most people with their individual ways of being can flourish. During the early stages of any group the facilitator has the unique opportunity to encourage the group to explore and adopt a set of norms which will help everyone. These include:

Encouraging people to listen to one another, to share experiences and to give each other feedback.

To nurture an accepting as well as a challenging atmosphere.

These can be more readily achieved if we adopt the following basic principles in our practice:

Help people to speak about their own experiences directly and in the first person.

Nurture fairness and evenhandedness in the interaction between group members.

Make positive space for silent group members. A group may learn as much from listening to someone's silence as it does from listening to speech.

Adjust the pace of the group in response to people's needs.
Foster an atmosphere in which people can take responsibility for
their actions and omissions.

Raise neglected or hidden issues when these do seem to be an
important part of the agenda.

Cultivate a reflective attitude to the process of the group.

Attempt to be open and tolerant, but above all truthful.

When a group undertakes creative-expressive work, by making paintings or sculptures, writing or by doing drama, the following may help
the nurturance of group members' freedom of expression:

The free-flow of ideas and associations is stimulated. Early
judgment of any ideas as either better or worse, acceptable or
unacceptable is actively discouraged. Every contribution matters
and is valued for what it is.

A climate is fostered in which difference is enjoyed. Similarities
and differences between various ways of coping are recognised as a
source of stimulation. When commonality occurs it is noted, but
not necessarily praised.

Prescriptive answers and solutions to the experienced problems are
avoided. It is taken as given that each of us has to find our own
specific way through, a way which is right for us.

Genuine, warm interest in one another's work is encouraged.
Praise or criticism of the formal quality of someone's contribution
is limited. What truly matters is the 'how' and to a lesser extent
the 'what'.

The courage which most of us need in order to express ourselves is
acknowledged and supported.

Especially during the early stages of the groupwork, every member
receives an equal share of time and attention.

These aspects of facilitator style create a climate in which group
members are able to take risks and try out new attitudes or ideas. Soon
people will find themselves speaking thoughts which until then had
been kept inside, covered with hesitance and the fear of being thought
peculiar. Once we open up, we are more likely to acknowledge that we
are also reluctant to change. We can then seek support when the going is
not easy – when our motivation dwindles amidst the demands of
everyday life or is weakened by the pressures from people who are also
important to us, but who happen to honour a different set of priorities.

Our honesty and developing trust then help us to recognise as well as
respect our own timidity. We see more clearly that from time to time we

are tired of having to adjust, that the struggle we face is often intimidating. Then we can admit to our fear of fighting the alarming rate of deforestation, the ruthless proliferation of nuclear weapons, or the illegal trade in threatened plant and animal species. Allowing ourselves to get worried. Once worried, we are more likely to understand 'what' we are up against and therefore infinitely more likely to be successful in bringing about change.

PART II
THE STORIES

ONE

AND SO IT CAME TO BE

The fig tree putteth forth her green figs
and the vines with the tender grape give a good smell.
Arise, my love, my fair one, and come away.
Song of Songs

Change is not necessarily all that it has been made out to be. Asking for help is not easy. To admit to shortcomings can be a positive embarrassment, whilst it demands more than a little bit of courage to admit that we are the cause as well as the victims of misfortune. Of course we were not promised a rose garden when we came to this earth. But equally we had not necessarily bargained for the reality that life also offers one difficulty after another. It promises to remain so.

And supposing that we were willing to change, then what . . . ? The people we love do not necessarily appreciate our efforts or join us on the journey. More often than not we shall find ourselves isolated and bewildered. Are these suitable rewards for the willingness to change?

Yet, how to give form to the restlessness which from time to time stirs within us like a distant yearning for a life with greater fulfilment, deeper resonance? Why do we sometimes feel so appallingly shallow? Guilty, nearly, as if the promise we made to ourselves is quietly but continuously betrayed. We, who once longed for passionate commitment now shy away from celebration, cowering in the dusty corners of complacency whenever we are called upon to protect more than our self-interest.

Where did our anger go? Our outrage? The wish to understand ourselves and others has not necessarily diminished. We still want to discover the reasons behind the particular effect which the environment has upon us and which we have upon the environment. But the desire for action is in danger of becoming submerged beneath the need for reprieve from anxiety, regrets and sorrow. With every new ecological disaster the internal urge to protect the last remaining wildernesses on earth from further devastation, paradoxically seems to wilt. Not to increase. How to understand such perplexing passivity? Randomly we move from one explanation of the meaning of events to another. Releasing a tension here or there. With cautious reserve we try to account for the real motivations which lie behind the way we feel. Meanwhile the world as we knew it is slipping away at terrifying speed. Of course we realise that we should be alarmed about atmospheric pollution; the devastation of the rainforests; drought, famine and dwindling rivers; the population explosion; and species extermination.

We are alarmed. At last something hopefully gets through to us. Touches us to the core. We are shaken into awareness. Maybe it was the expression in the otter's eyes, or the call of dying seal-puppies, or the eagle who flapped helpless wings above an empty nest. Then, like lovers still scarred by betrayal and deception, we tentatively re-explore the variety of life which is ours to cherish.

We discern that a great deal has already been lost and that much more will be lost unless we accept that in spite of our felt powerlessness, we exercise a crucial influence on the development and survival of eco-systems. Sooner or later we must concede that the relentless pressure which we feel 'within' bears similarities to the relentless pressure exercised 'without' through the unceasing acceleration of tourism, and industrial and agricultural development. We know that our internal as well as our external resources are threatened. Over-exploitation lurks everywhere. We have to rethink terms such as the use and misuse of natural resources, compelled to become conscious of what we do and don't do. We appreciate that the art of protection and the art of prudent management must be set against the desire for instant gratification, the pain of waiting and our intolerance of ambiguity.

The nature of the trouble is presented to us by the troubles of nature. The methods by which fundamental improvements can be brought about escape us at this stage of the process. Seeing more clearly how we could tinker in the margin. Images of the desired change appear and disappear. Somehow we need to acquire an internal locus of strength and organisation. Our affective considerations must be expressed and combine with our cognitive considerations to prod us into action. Once more we desire to make our influence felt. With our strength nourished, we dare to assume a new habit of confidence and authority. Yes, it could all have been so much better if we had acted earlier. We didn't. That is all there is to it. The unlived past demands to be mourned. The unlived future needs to be mourned. When we acknowledge our frailty as well as our need for companionship and support, real change may well be possible. With this belief and supported by such intentions we join an action group or a personal development group. Preparing and pruning ourselves for a greener world.

1 How the earth was made

IN THE BEGINNING Maheo, the great spirit, lived in the great emptiness. He looked and there was nothing. He opened his ears and there was nothing. He knew himself to be Maheo, the one who is by himself in nothingness. His powers were many and therefore Maheo was not lonesome in his aloneness. Was not his being a universe? The never-ending time of nothingness became his space and he moved through it stirring his thoughts. He wondered what his power could do. Then he thought: 'Is my power of any use, if I do not make a world and people to live there?' He told his power to create salty water so that all life might come from this. In the long-ago darkness Maheo felt the water and he tasted the salt on his lips.

Then Maheo spoke to his power commanding it to create the water-beings. They came to be. First the fish which swim in the water, then the shellfish and other creatures of the sea. Some of these made their home in the mud which Maheo had made so the water would have a bottom. Then Maheo again spoke with his power and asked that there might be creatures that lived on the water. They came to be. There were snowgeese and mallards and teal and coots and terns and loons. In the great darkness Maheo could hear how they splashed in the water.

Then Maheo's desire made him wish to see what he had made. And indeed so it came to be. Slowly the first light spread across the earth and Maheo saw his creation. He knew its beauty. Then a bird talked to him, saying: 'I wonder where you are, you who made us. I know not who you are, but I know that you are out there somewhere. Listen to us, Maheo. You have granted us much that is good. The water is a great gift. But we birds cannot live as the fish live. We like paddling and drifting on the water. But there are also times when we do not want to be bound to the water, we so much want to leave it then. Even though we know not how or where.' Maheo stretched his hands towards the birds. He moved his fingers like the flapping of wings and soon the birds could fly. For a while it seemed as if the skies were darkened by the flurry of their wings. Maheo thought: 'How beautiful they are,' and from that time onwards birds could fly or swim as they choose.

The loon let himself float on the water, for he was tired. He knew that Maheo was very near him. He said quietly: 'We have the water, the sky, light and now we can also fly. It is not good to ask for more, but maybe it is, for when the swimming and flying are done, we so much want a place where we can make a nest. Could you please make us such a place, Maheo?'

Maheo agreed with the loon. He said: 'My power made water, light, air and the peoples of the water. I now need your help to continue creation, for I was only able to make four things by myself alone.' The waterpeople spoke as if in one voice: 'Please, tell us how.'

'We must find land,' Maheo said. The snowgoose came and offered to be the first one who would try and find land. She flew high into the sky. Then she dived deep into the water. She was gone a long time. She returned, sighing: 'I have brought nothing.' Then the loon flew high into the sky, dived deep into the water and was gone a long, long time. He returned and whispered so that only Maheo heard him: 'I too brought nothing.' The third to try was the mallard. He brought nothing either.

At last the little coot came forward, saying hesitantly: 'Maybe there is nothing down below, but sometimes when I look down in the water, I think that I see something. Snowgoose, Loon and Mallard

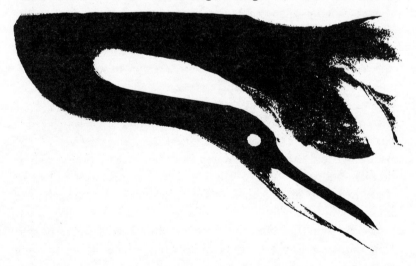

tried to dive. Shall I swim to where I think the mud is and see if I can bring something back? I shall do my best. Could I please try, Maheo?' Maheo answered: 'Little brother coot, we can all only do our best. We cannot do more. Try swimming, it might work out better than diving. Try, little coot, and see what happens.'

Coot was gone for a long, long, long, long time. Then Maheo and snowgoose, loon and mallard and all the waterpeople saw something rise in the waters. It was Coot. He was very tired. The water lifted him to the surface, gently, so gently. Coot stretched his little beak towards the light. He did not open it. Only when Maheo asked, did he open it. There was a tiny bit of mud. It rolled onto Maheo's hand. Maheo thanked little coot saying: 'What you have brought us, will always be your protection.' This has happened. Because coot's flesh still tastes like mud, people and animals only eat coot when they are very, very hungry.

Maheo held the mud between the palms of his hands and it grew. Again he asked for help for he needed to put the mud somewhere. It had to be on the back of one of the waterpeople. They all offered to carry the mud, but some were too small, others too narrow. At last Maheo asked Grandmother Turtle. She said: 'I'm old Maheo, remember that, and not very quick. But like little coot, I'll try.'

Then Maheo used Grandmother Turtle's back to start building the mud. It grew and he made hills and plains and valleys. Soon Grandmother Turtle could no longer be seen. Since that time turtles have been at home in the waters, on earth and within the ground. They walk or swim, whatever they like. This is because Grandmother Turtle carries the earth on her back. It was this way. It is this way.

Maheo saw the barren earth. Once more he asked his power to help him, for he wanted the earth to be fruitful. To nourish life. Soon seeds and grass and flowers and trees blossomed. Birds came and rested in their midst. They built their nests and the earth was beautiful. Maheo knew its beauty. Then Maheo made people from his ribs. He made two of them for he knew that it is not good for people to be alone. He watched them together with Grandmother Earth. They were their children: hers and his.

In the springtime people's children were born and more children were born. From time to time Maheo created animals. The people and the animals lived with each other and for each other. He also made the Buffalo. Maheo is always with us. He watches this good creation. We are all here because of Maheo, the Great Spirit, whose thoughts stirred in nothingness.

2   In the dreamtime lived Tiddalik, the frog

IN THE DREAMTIME there lived a frog called Tiddalik. He was a very big frog. As big as a mountain. When he walked he crushed trees and plants under his enormous webbed feet. Tiddalik, the frog, was thirsty. Because he was so big and so thirsty, he started to drink the rain which fell from the sky. He just opened his mouth as wide as he could. From that time onwards all the rain was drunk by Tiddalik. But this was not enough. He was still thirsty. He looked at the pools, the rivulets, the streams. He wanted more fresh water. Then he drank. Every last drop of sweet water on earth was drunk by Tiddalik.

It had been the dry season but soon the animals of the dreamtime noticed that something strange was happening. It was as if someone was drinking all the water. This someone was Tiddalik. He drank and he drank and still he felt thirsty.

The animals became very frightened. They saw that the plants and the trees were dying of thirst. The drought was killing everything whilst Tiddalik was growing bigger and bigger. All of the water of the world was now inside him and he would not let go of any of it.

The animals called a meeting to discuss what they had to do. Some said that Tiddalik was far too big and powerful. He would never give the water back. Others said, that it was all just terrible, terrible. Some wanted to give up and die. Then wise old Wombat spoke. He took a step forward into the circle of animals, saying: 'I have an idea. We should try to make Tiddalik laugh. Then all the water will come out of his mouth. It will just spout out of his mouth. We must try and make him laugh.'

The animals agreed with Wombat. This was a good idea. They could try and make Tiddalik, the great frog, laugh.

They went to the place where Tiddalik lived. He did not even look at the amazing trail of animals. He sat there, his enormous belly swollen with water. Kookaburra had offered to begin. He did all he could to make Frog laugh. But Frog did not even smile a little. He took no notice whatsoever of poor Kookaburra.

Then Kangeroo tried. Hopping and jumping and falling about in funny ways. But Tiddalik, the frog, just sat there. His puffed-up face as frozen as stone. Then Lizard tried. It must be said that he did his best. He performed the strangest tricks to make Tiddalik laugh. But the frog did not blink and he kept his mouth tightly closed.

At last Nabunum, the eel, came forward. The drought had made him too come on to the land. He had been in search of water when he chanced across the great meeting of animals. He slid across the scorched earth until he was near Wombat, for he had a very soft voice. Then Nabunum said: 'I am a stranger in your midst. But may I try.' The animals agreed. Kookaburra, Kangeroo, and Lizard had done their best but Frog had not looked them in the eye, let alone laughed. Maybe this strange eel could do the trick.

Nabunum carefully chose his place. Not too near and not too far away. He returned Frog's stare with a steady gaze and he slowly raised himself off the ground. Did he see something tremble near Frog's big lips? Nabunum began to sway. It was the beginning of his dance. At first he danced gently and calmly, then wilder and wilder. He twisted and turned and moved himself into the funniest shapes of the world.

Frog's eyes gleamed with reluctant pleasure. He held his belly for he did not want to laugh. But Nabunum jumped about and wriggled and squirmed. Then suddenly Frog's big mouth opened. He laughed the greatest laugh. As he laughed all the waters of the world gushed out. Big streams of clear, beautiful water. Every rivulet and pond and stream was at once filled with sweet, clear water. The plants did grow again and the animals were no longer thirsty.

It had been Wombat's idea. It happened in the dreamtime.

3   When the sky-opening was found

IN THE OLD DAYS Kaboi, the big one, knew in his heart a great many things. The people made him their chief. Kaboi's people lived in the village which is to this very day below our own world. All kinds of plants grew in that underground world. There were also birds and beasts. The early people had not yet discovered our world; they did not know that it existed. They were happy where they lived.

Then, one day, Kaboi heard the song of a bird. Never before in his life had he heard such beautiful bird-song. It seemed as if the bird was calling him. It cried: 'Follow me, follow me.' Kaboi could not help himself. He gathered some people and all of them went in pursuit of the bird. Further and further away from their village they went, never losing sight of the bird which sang urgently: 'Come, follow me.'

At last they came to where they had never been before. In that place there was an opening which was above them. That bird flew into the sky-opening and disappeared. The people wondered what to do. They could still hear the bird's lingering call and they wanted to travel to where it had gone. Then the people of the ancient time climbed into the opening, but Kaboi could not follow them for he was too big. Kaboi did not like it that he could not join his people on their journey through the sky-opening. He did not like it at all. He asked the people to travel through the sky-opening to the place which he knew to be up there, to look around carefully and then to come back and speak of all that they had seen.

Kaboi sat down near the place of the sky-opening and he waited.

The people of the ancient time climbed through the sky-opening and walked about on earth. They opened their eyes to our animals, the rivers and rocks, to wild honey, ripe and unripe fruits, and to the rotten wood of dying trees. They picked up a marvellous piece of wood which they wanted to show Kaboi for they did not know what it was. Then they found the sky-opening again and made their way down to their own world. Kaboi was still waiting for them. Though much time had passed he had not aged, for that is how it was in the world below.

The people spoke with great delight of the land where they had feasted on all kinds of food and where all had danced before their eyes in myriad shapes and forms. They also showed Kaboi their piece of wood. It glowed and they asked him what it was. He held it in his hands, looking at it with great intent. It seemed as if he had to strengthen his breath. Then he told the people about the death of trees. They looked at Kaboi, the big one. Immediately they were struck by the knowing that all living beings were like trees. Even people were like trees, and that therefore people too would die in the world which was above their own.

When the people who travelled through the sky-opening came home they told the other villagers all that had happened. They described our world's beauty and manifold blessings. But they did not talk about death.

At once the village-people of the old time wanted to get ready and travel to the land of the bird's calling.

Kaboi pleaded for silence. He showed them the piece of rotten wood. The ancient people did not understand him. They merely saw the wood's glowing beauty. Kaboi, however, spoke of death and dying. They did not grasp what he said. Most villagers left their world that time. They came to our world and found that it was greatly blessed. They also found death. We all die.

In the world below Kaboi and his people are still alive. Their strength has not been diminished. The sky-opening has been forever closed. It had to be that way.

4 Coyote steals the fire

IN THE BEGINNING people were new to this world. During summer, when the sun warmed their land and the nights were mild, they lived contentedly. But summer never lasted. Autumn and then winter came. Cold stretched across the earth and the fierce, distant sparkle of the stars in the night-sky frightened the early people. Would the sun ever return? Thus when the plants were dressed in hoar-frost the people huddled together. Holding one another tight

they wished that the frozen days would end. They cried because
spring never came soon enough and they never held one another
tight enough. Each winter people died. Old and sick or young and
weak the fierce winter-cold embraced these fragile ones beyond the
people's terrified grasp. Then they chanted their plaints of grief.
Another winter and another death.

In that time, Coyote, the bringer-of-much, wandered the earth.
He felt great sorrow for the people of newness. He could not give
them the fur they so wanted. This was not good. He therefore
thought of something he could give. He knew that a long way away
on a distant mountaintop three fire-people lived who jealously
guarded the only fire in the world. Fire which could give the people

the warmth they needed. But these fire-beings kept watch so carefully that no one had ever been able to take some fire away from them.

Coyote, the bringer-of-much, spoke to his old knowing. Then he wandered to the fire-beings' mountain. He came when darkness was about to fall. He watched. A silent shadow of the forest he was, a mere grey coyote at one with his watching.

Safely covered by dense bushes, he saw how the fire-beings gazed at their fire. From time to time they suddenly looked round and hurt the forest with their sparkling furious eyes. Always dreading that some-one might come and take the fire which they wanted to be theirs alone. Coyote watched for a long, long time. Night went and day came and another night and another day, until he knew with all his knowing how the fire-people guarded their fire.

Then he left, a mere grey coyote slinking off. He went deep into the forest and called towards himself the animals who were also touched by the frozen people's sorrow: the furry animals, the ones with feathers and those with thick skins.

They came and heard Coyote's tale. They did not really need his words, for they too had listened to the people's plaint of grief. As soon as Coyote told the animals about the jealous fire-beings, they promised their help.

So it came to be that at that time, in the beginning when people were new to this world, Coyote returned to the far-distant mountain. Once more he became a shadow to his own darkness and he waited. It was the time of dusk when he arrived. It was the time of dawn, when the fire-beings changed their watch as usual, that Coyote lunged forward. He snatched a glowing bundle of fire.

Then he rushed down the mountain side. The sky filled with the fire-beings rage. They howled and ran after him. One of them caught his tail, which is why Coyote's tail is still white today, but Coyote flung the fire far away. It was Squirrel who caught it. She had known where to wait for Coyote and she was there. She put the fire on her back and ran. Her back was sorely scorched by the fire and even now her tail curls to cover the place of wounding. The fire-beings nearly caught Squirrel with the fire, but she threw it to Chipmunk, who was also clawed by the fire-beings. She was clawed badly. They tore three stripes down her back. The stripes tell us of Chipmunk's courage. The fire-beings nearly caught the fire that time for Chipmunk's pain was great, but Frog too was in his place of waiting. Chipmunk threw the fire towards him. The fire-beings fell upon Frog and tore at his tail. With all his strength Frog jumped away. He lost his tail, which is why frogs do not have tails even today, and he jumped, jumped away.

But the fire-beings followed him too. Then Frog cast the fire to the trees. And the trees swallowed it. They just swallowed it. The fire could no longer be seen. The fire-beings looked and begged and pleaded and promised, but the forest had swallowed the fire and the trees did not relent.

Coyote, the bringer-of-much, asked the trees about the fire. They told him and he told the people of the days of newness. He showed them the trick of rubbing sticks together to make fire and the trick of spinning a sharp stick in a wooden hole.

In this manner the people received the gift of fire. Coyote, the bringer-of-much, he made this happen.

5   A name for a cat

A COURT DIGNITARY by the name of Chi was the owner of a remarkably beautiful cat. The cat was a great source of pride for the man. He therefore called the cat Tiger.

One day he invited some friends to visit his home. The conversation soon turned to the cat's name. One of the guests said: 'It is true that a tiger is fierce, but he is not as fierce as a dragon nor as powerful. Maybe the cat's name should have been Dragon.'

'I do concede that the dragon is more powerful than the tiger,' another guest added, 'but a dragon has to make an effort to reach the clouds. It is obvious that clouds are more elevated than dragons. I suggest that you rename your cat and call him Cloud.'

Another guest spoke immediately: 'Of course clouds may cover the entire sky. However, even a tiny breeze sets clouds moving. A little wind disperses them and nothing can make the clouds resist his power. I advice you, call him Wind.'

The fourth guest raised his eyebrows. Smiling benignly, he said: 'And where are the powers of wind – which I admit, deserve to be respected – when it meets a stone wall? The correct name for this cat is 'Wall.'

'A wall is made to resist the wind,' said the fifth guest, 'but even a little mouse can gnaw a hole in a wall. It is self-evident that your cat needs to be called Mouse.'

An old man from the village, Chuang-Li, listened to the guests. He said mockingly: 'Who kills the mouse?'

6 Lifting the sky

THE WORLD WAS FIRST MADE in the east. Then He-Who-Makes and He-Who-Changes slowly travelled west. They made all the earth's creatures as they travelled along. The people of the places through which they passed received their own language. There were many people and many languages. When He-Who-Makes and He-Who-Changes came to Puget-Sound they came home. They were wearied with travel. They therefore took their bag of languages and strewed it around this place. Because there were still so many different languages in the bag the people who lived near Puget-Sound each got their very own language and therefore they had great trouble knowing what the others said.

In spite of this the people soon discovered how angry everyone was that the sky was so very low. It was just above their heads. They only had to climb into a tree to bump against it. Of course He-Who-Makes and He-Who-Changes did not want them to bump their heads against the sky. So they were not allowed to climb trees. But some people did it anyway. These people learned the language of the Skyworld and they disappeared up there.

Each tribe had wise people. One day these wise people called a meeting to talk about the sky being so low. They really did not like it. They wanted to lift the sky. After much time had passed they thought that if they all tried to work together, they might be able to lift the sky.

One of them said: 'We can do it. We must all push. All the creatures of the world, the animals, the birds, the insects and the people, must push the sky away.' They talked and with their far-seeing-eyes they saw how every being of the world would be there at that time and push. Then one of them said: 'We will all push when we feel like it. This will not be good. We speak in different ways. How can it not be so?' The wise people thought and talked and pondered. Then this one said: 'We can know the time to push. We know if we listen to each other. "Yaa-hoooh" is the sound for pushing. Let this be the sound which will tell us, now is the time for pushing together.' They all agreed.

Then the wise people spoke with those to whom they belonged. They told them about the sky-lifting day. Each one of them guided their people to a tall tree. The tree was asked if it wanted to become a sky-lifting pole. If the tree agreed to be made into a pole it was cut down.

Time passed and the sky-lifting day arrived. All the earth's peoples were in their place. They lifted their poles and the sky had all these poles against it. Then they-who-were-gathered shouted 'Yaa-hoooh' and the pushing began. They pushed and shouted 'Yaa-hoooh' many times. The sky was lifted. It was lifted to the place where it is now.

No one has bumped their head against the sky since that time and no one has entered the Skyworld either.

Working with the stories

How the earth was made

I NEED YOUR HELP

Think of a word which you associate with the word 'help'.

Share your word association with the group.

After having listened to all the associations, select one which resonates most with you. This may be your own word.

Using finger paints – paint the image evoked by this word.

Find a partner.

Talk about the feelings/memories evoked by your paintings. Then list the kind of situations which might have made you use the sentence: 'Can I give you a hand?' E.g. carrying someone's luggage; opening a tin of sardines; or pushing a car with engine trouble off the road.

Return to the circle.

Invite everyone to mention one of these situations.

Tell the story 'How the earth was made'.

Encourage group members to doodle whilst the story of Maheo is told.

Decide which character you like. Then select a moment in the story which made a particular impression upon you. Write about this scene from your character's point of view. Make use of his/her ideas, memories and comments. This task is made easier if you begin your writing with 'I . . . '

Share your writings with each other.

RESPONSE TASK: create as many small pieces of paper as there are group members. When a person has finished reading, record which quality you really appreciate in their character. Give your paper to the group member concerned. The gifts won't be read until all the writings have been shared. Note: if for whatever reason a group member chooses not to write or to share, ask the group members to create a gift for an unknown creature. Hand these gifts to the non-disclosing group member.

Read the gifts you have received.

Select one or two which feel particularly important to you.

Share what you have chosen with the group.

Reflect upon the entire session.

In the dreamtime lived Tiddalik, the frog
PERSPECTIVES ON THIRST AND GREED

Ask group members to share what they enjoy or used to enjoy drinking, from buttermilk or apple juice to lager, champagne and coffee. Recall as many types of drink as possible, including the more obscure ones. Talk a little about these preferences/memories.

Recall a time when you felt really thirsty. Share your experience with the people on your left and right.

Ask yourself what your overriding emotion was. What did it feel like to be quite so thirsty? What would the feeling have turned into if you had no prospect of being able to quench your thirst for quite some time? Decide upon a feeling-word, e.g. frightened, furious, totally self-centred.

Ask your partner(s) to adopt a posture which portrays this feeling word. If necessary adjust the posture until you are satisfied that it adequately reflects your word.

Share these 'feeling-word' sculptures with the entire group.

Reflect on the body-sculptures and the feelings evoked.

Tell the story of 'Tiddalik the Frog'.

Imagine that some time *after* Tiddalik released the water, the animals call a council-meeting. The drought has finished, but Tiddalik is still living in their midst. Some animals feel that:

> Tiddalik should be punished for the trouble he caused.
>   (If so, how . . . ?)
> Tiddalik should be re-educated.
>   (If so, how . . . ?)
> Nothing should be done at all. There isn't a problem.

Remind group members that the animal council is accustomed to resolving such issues in a spirit of co-operation and kindness.

Invite group members to choose which animal character they would like to represent. Then, which line of argument they want to pursue. Preferably one which is dissimilar from their usual position.

Introduce yourself 'as the animal you will play' to the animal council meeting. Discuss Tiddalik's future and try to reach a decision which meets with everyone's approval. The role play will run for at most fifteen minutes. Please inform group members when there are five more minutes left.

Walk around the room and ponder what happened to you in role as one of the dreamtime animals. Did you say anything which you want to ponder at great length? Or did you *not* say something whilst in role which you feel should have been said? Does this give you food for thought?

Return to the circle.

Share your experiences in the animal council.

Reflect on the process by which your group achieved a resolution, or on the process by which your group did *not* achieve a resolution.

Make some connections between the story, the role play and your actual life experience.

Select one issue/question/theme to which you need to give some attention at a later stage. Especially any issues evoked by the thirst-work early on during the session.

Reflect upon the entire session.

When the sky-opening was found

WE TRAVEL TOWARDS NEWNESS

Warm up body and voice through various follow-the-leader movement/sound imitation exercises.

Explore together in pairs different ways of travelling from A to B in the room: e.g. crawling, running, carrying your partner, etc.

Join with another pair. Show what you have done. Share each other's ways of travelling.

Find a new partner: discover which place each of you has visited, which the other person has not been to. Establish which two places these are.

Talk for two minutes each. Each partner in turn describes this place with as much detail as possible. The other partner just listens.

In movement, enact your partner's exploration of this place. Try not to fill gaps in the information you were given. Rely on what you have been told. When both places have been explored through movement, discuss what this has evoked for you.

Return to the circle.

Tell the story 'When the sky-opening was found'.

Write a number above five but below fifty on a piece of paper.

Imagine that you are one of the villagers who left the old world. Some time has passed. The number you have just written down represents this person's current age. Decide whether your character is male or female. You want to write Kaboi a letter to tell him about your life in the new world. About the good and the not so good times. Write this letter.

RESPONSE TASK: collect and redistribute these letters. Imagine that you are Kaboi. You have received a letter. Read it and write a reply. Return the 'new world' letter plus Kaboi's response to the original author.

Read the response which you have received.

Share your own letter, plus Kaboi's response, with the group.

Make connections between these letters and your own life experience.

Reflect upon the entire session.

Coyote steals the fire

WE DISCOVER WARMTH

Play 'off-ground tig'. The purpose of the game is for group members to avoid being caught by the person who is 'it'. Scatter some cushions, boxes or old newspapers around the room. To avoid being caught a player has to get on to one of these. They can only stay off the ground for a count of three. Play until group is warmed up.

Walk around the room and focus on your breath. Notice how it slowly returns to normal. Breathe quietly and deeply. Notice too the warmth in your arms and legs. Then let your mind wander towards feeling cold. Think of times that you have felt cold. Maybe it rained and a fierce wind blew. Maybe it happened during a spell of freezing weather or when you didn't have enough blankets to keep you warm. Think too about times when the weather was fine, but you felt cold inside. Move very slowly and stiffly. Imagine that the cold has really entered your body.

Stop walking. Don't move. Gradually make eye contact with the person(s) nearest to you and, very slowly, begin a shared, frozen dance. Do not touch. Focus your awareness on being frozen into near immobility and yet experiencing the desire to make contact.

End your dance.

Breathe on to your hands. Feel the warmth of your breath. Then rub your hands together. Stamp your feet and with your partner(s) begin a vigorous rhythm-beating/clapping/stamping game. Use your own body/their body to make rhythmical clapping sounds. Thighs/buttocks/and the tops of shoulders make good body-drums.

Sit down after a while and share your experiences around the theme of 'feeling cold'.

Paint a small image of a landscape.

Quickly record your answers to the following questions:

> What kind of a landscape is it?
> Suppose that somewhere in this landscape all the warmth that exists had been hidden. Where has it been hidden?
> Why can't anyone get near it?
> Who decides to try and get it, so that the warmth can again be distributed?
> Which difficulty has to be overcome?
> Who or what enables a successful outcome?
> How is the warmth maintained?
> Who or what ensures that warmth will always be available?

Write your story.

Share the stories you have written.

RESPONSE TASK: while listening to the stories, create a painting which reflects the images evoked in you.

Hand your painting to one of the group members. Ensure that everyone receives a painting.

Tell the story 'Coyote Steals the Fire'.

Look at the painting you have received, remind yourself of the stories, and think of some words of encouragement for a cold person. Write these on the painting and return it to the person who gave it to you.

Share these words of encouragement with the group.

Reflect upon the entire session.

A *name for a cat*

ME AND MY NAME

Play 'One, two, three'. Group members stand in a circle. Try to make eye contact with one another. Count in unison 'one, two, three'. Those people who at the count of three have eye contact with one another, swap places. Repeat counting/swapping places several times.

Tell the story 'A name for a cat'.

Reflect a little on the story.

Make a huge, silent yawn. Then yawn with a soft sound, a louder one. Then very noisily, then more softly, etc. until the yawning stops.

Talk in pairs. Decide who will go first/second. Each person will have five minutes to talk about their name(s):

How were you given your name?

What do you like/dislike about it? Is there another name you would have preferred?

Do you know other people who have the same name? Any feelings about them?

Do you have a 'special' name? Are you willing to share it?

Write your name on a large sheet of paper. With your partner's help, record on this sheet several of the comments you have made. Then distribute the sheets of paper randomly. Continue to work in the same pairs.

RESPONSE TASK: read the notes which you have received. Imagine that you are a gifted poet and have been asked to compose a poem or love-song for someone who has this name. The notes you have just received are all the information you have. You write this poem/song.

Share this poem with your partner. She/he will present your poem/song to the group. Rehearse the performance.

Share your performance.

Return to your partner.

Talk about the impact of the performances. Connect your response to the cat story with your response to the poem/song based around your name. Select an aspect of these experiences which you wish to remember.

Return to the circle.

Share your experiences and particularly the aspects you wish to remember.

Reflect on the entire session.

Lifting the sky

TOO LITTLE SPACE

Stand or sit in a circle:

Focus on breathing out. Breathe in and again focus on breathing out. Then begin to hum. At first softly, then somewhat louder, then softly again.

In pairs: hum cheek to cheek, forehead to forehead. Try to feel the humming vibrations.

Talk with your partner about the experience.

Return to the circle.

Tell the story 'Lifting the sky'.

Write on a large sheet of paper words/feelings/images associated with 'Too little space'. List as many of these as possible.

Select one of these.

Use finger paints to create the image evoked by the word/image you have chosen. Then . . .

Take a paper and pen. Quickly answer the following questions (record your answers very briefly):

> What is the landscape/environment?
> Who or what lives in this environment?
> In what kind of a dwelling-place?
> Why is there too little space in this dwelling-place?
> Why is this particularly difficult?
> What makes matters worse?
> Which solution is tried?
> Why does it fail?
> Who or what comes to the rescue?
> How is the situation ultimately resolved?

Write your story on the basis of your answers to the questions.

Share your stories.

RESPONSE TASK: make sure you have as many small pieces of paper as there are group members. When you have listened to a story, create a small gift for the main character in that story. Write the name of the story's author on the back of your gift. Once everyone has shared their tale, distribute the gifts.

Open your gifts.

Select one or two which you are particularly pleased to accept on behalf of your character.

Reflect upon the entire session.

A few questions to explore

○ What are the differences and similarities between the process of creation suggested in the story 'How the earth was made' and the process of creation as described by evolution theory?

○ What are the functions of mud?

○ What kind of life exists in water?

○ Why did the buffalo disappear from the North American plains?

○ How do different birds rest?

○ Look at various birds' flying and diving patterns. What are the differences/similarities?

○ Why does Australia have some special kinds of animals? Which ones are they?

○ What is drought? What causes a drought and what are its consequences?

○ How do frogs drink?

○ How do animals communicate with each other? What kind of signals/sounds are used? Can this be called speech or even a language?

○ How do animals such as the kookaburra, kangaroo, lizard and eel move about? What is special about these particular animals?

○ What is a tropical rainforest?

○ What is the most enchanting bird-song you have ever heard?

○ What is special about the rainforest canopy?

○ What is death and what causes it?

○ Why are the processes of decay and rot so important?

○ What exactly is fire and which different ways of starting a fire do you know/can you use?

○ Which gases do various fires produce? Why are some of these a threat?

o What is the function of names?

o When can a language be called a language and when is it a dialect? How many languages exist?

o What is the sky? How come we see the sky as blue?

o How do people learn to co-operate?

TWO

IT WAS A WOUNDED CRY

I stepped from plank to plank
A slow and cautious way;
The stars about my head I felt,
About my feet the sea.
EMILY DICKINSON

When we first join a new group, we bring to the experience a wide range of longings and anxieties. Memories of other groups loom large. Shall we simply repeat patterns of interaction? Or will this group be different? Might we be able to develop relationships in unexpected ways? We have made a commitment to change. We want things to improve and know that therefore contentious differences between ourselves and others have to be acknowledged and reduced. How to differentiate between the contentious ones and those we need to learn to value? Apathy and fragmentation, which paralysed us for so long, must slowly and gradually be replaced by a growing appreciation of the total energy which a group can command, the synergy.

In the groups which we joined as a result of our renewed 'commitment to commitment', we soon witness how difficult it can be to tolerate painful insight. How substantial the longing is to pretend that this pain does not really exist, or that it need not last very long. The desire to close the door on uncomfortable self-realisations looms large. But because most group members feel that the Rubicon has been crossed, the wish to deny is balanced by an equally strong wish to explore and face the facts.

During the early stages of group formation some members will probably urge the group towards immediate rational attempts at problem solving. Their reality orientation is inspired by the wish to avoid the mistakes made elsewhere of having wasted valuable time through internecine conflict and the seemingly pointless harking back to minor irritations and frustrations. This process of pushing for immediate solutions is often supported by the shared commitment to make change happen. The group experiences substantial act-hunger. Consequently there is pressure to bring the group together quickly. To gloss over differences in the aid of a barely conscious yearning for sameness.

Therefore this is also a dangerous stage for the group. At best people are offered a unique opportunity to negotiate and accommodate differences. At worst uniqueness is denied and 'the different ones' sooner rather than later drop out. At this stage we witness in some groups lengthy discussions, during which it is propounded that everyone must take equal responsibility. Do their bit. Equality matters. Tasks have to be evenly distributed or at least fairly distributed according to strength and available resources. These discussions may well serve the useful function of slowing the process down a bit, forestalling the implementation of early and ill-considered change.

Whenever we join a new group our spoken or unspoken expectations tend to be high: more often, than not, unrealistically so. Yet such expectations are the fuel which initially motivates the group to work.

Sadly the process of letting go of these early expectations is frequently confused with the voiced perception that group members avoid real change because they wish to postpone action. We hear it said that there is no time to lose and note that tension in the group is rising due to the emergence of fight-flight patterns in members' ways of coping with disappointment. Arguments emerge between gradualists and radicalists. Pairing happens. In order to strengthen their power base couples are formed. Sometimes triangles. Even during this early phase of the group's work it is posited that some people should re-examine their commitment. Some suggest that maybe the groupwork does not suit them. However, it is more likely that in its blind urge towards sameness, such people do not suit the group. Because they signify the difference: difference which feels uncomfortable. Consequently the danger is that the outsider, the loner, is manoeuvred towards an even more marginal position within the group. If the group succeeds at losing such a member, it will take quite a blow. For sooner or later people will realise that the presence of healthy difference is fundamental to the group's long-term survival.

A few weeks into the group many people appear to be riding a much-loved high horse. It is surprising to recall that only a week earlier we may have felt optimistic about this very same group of people, noting that they seemed really together. Then the fourth or fifth session arrived and without any explanation attendance dropped. The atmosphere became tense. There are sudden barriers everywhere. Communication appears to break down on more than one occasion – whilst, paradoxically, most people seem to be trying to get a message across. Their message. There's talk about disappointment. The memory that only last week everyone was contented, drifts beyond reach.

To make matters worse we encounter a sudden abundance of ideas related to what this group ought to be doing and how it ought to be run. There appears to be a lively competition for leadership, though few would acknowledge this. Surprisingly, ignorance is running rife. Suggestions and counter-suggestions permeate the discussion. The flow of information has become somewhat manic. Meetings are like catalogues of self-surveys, which would not be so bad if they were leading somewhere. It does not appear that they do. The group is not only noticing the inadequacies of ways of perceiving and being. It is living them.

Maybe this is what is meant by change, for occasionally someone recognises that these ways of relating are outdated. Sometimes feedback about maladaptive segmentation can be given. The capacity to tolerate negative group phenomena is certainly developing. In fact it appears that the group is positively generating such experiences. We realise that the tendency towards pernicious internal conflict must be addressed: we do not wish to collude unwittingly with the subtle or not so subtle attempts to maintain the status quo. After the early bout of change-energy, there now seems to be a huge investment in no change behaviour. Of course the increased communication flow will sooner or later exert such pressure that change becomes unavoidable. In all likelihood the dissatisfaction with the actual situation is already mounting. The perceived discrepancy between how the group is functioning and how it could be operating, becomes distressing. Maybe there is a process at work. But if there is, someone had better explain the stages, so that the group can continue. Members are finding it hard to sustain the uncertainty, because every attempt at achieving premature solutions seems to be forestalled. It is said that change is not a straightforward process.

When, as is inevitable, the group comes to its senses, the members more often than not decide that they should just knuckle down and solve some of the small, immediate problems; intuitively realising that this will help the building of the capacity to deal with more important issues. Through such action the immediate survival needs of the group are addressed. A new internal structure is generated, not imposed. The first hurdle has been taken. The process continues.

1   Raven and the man who sat on the tide

I N THE EARLY DAYS there were no tides and no shallow waters, whilst the fish lived a long way from the land. Though the people had boats they had no fishing nets. The young men from the village dived to catch fish with their spears. Their catch was always small for the great waters were very cold. Because there was little other food the people went hungry. This pained the fishermen for they knew that there were fish in abundance. If only the fish swam nearer the land and did not have to live in such deep waters. They watched helplessly as their kinsfolk starved to death.

Because he liked people, Raven, the maker of many things, flew from village to village. He wanted to know what was happening to the world which he had made. He too saw that the people were suffering. During one of his visits the people told him about their trouble. Could he not find a way of bringing the fish closer to land? It was wrong that the water was so deep. Would he not be able to make it shallow in some places? Raven thought. When he had moulded the earth with mountains and creatures, with rivers and the wide ocean, he had finished as far as he was concerned. Now the people were asking him to do even more. He said: 'I don't know what I can do to help you.' The villagers were thrown by Raven's words. He was the maker of much and he did not know how to bring the fish nearer the shore?

Then an old woman stepped forward. She said: 'Raven, there lives a being far out at sea, who is ancient. None of us have ever met this one, but we know that it exists. We call it "Foggun". Maybe you could ask Foggun for help?' Raven looked at the old woman. He had no choice. Of course he had to try and find this Foggun.

Raven had been flying a long, long time when his wings were touched by great clouds of fog rolling thick and fast above the waters. Then he saw Foggun, the ancient one. After he had neatly folded his wings Raven greeted the fellow spirit from the time before time. Foggun did not move. Not knowing whether he was noticed or understood, Raven spoke about the frightened, hungry people.

People who died because the fish swam too deep in the ocean's belly. For their sake some of the fish had to come inland and move about in gentler, shallow water. Did Foggun know how this could be done? Could he offer help?

Foggun appeared neither to listen nor to care. Raven pleaded even more urgently. He needed guidance. Did Foggun not hear him? Raven the Creator was begging for help. The life of his people was at stake. How could the sea be given shallow places? Suddenly the ancient voice spoke about a giant who dwelled in the ocean's furthest reaches. This was the giant who sat on the tide. 'Tide . . . ' said Raven, 'What is a tide?' But Foggun could no longer be seen. Dense mist clouded Raven's eyes. He opened his ears even wider. Was there a final whisper of the ancient voice? But no sound trembled in that long ago time. Raven had to continue his search.

Again Raven, the maker of much, flew a long, long time. Just when he grew tired of flying, he saw in the distance the shape of a giant. He screeched with relief. The enormous face turned towards him. The giant's eyes did not look friendly. Unintimidated Raven spoke once again of people and mountains and hunger and of the urgent need for shallow waters. The giant too did not appear to listen. He mumbled in response: 'I am the man who sits on the tide. I have always sat on the tide.' Raven asked him about the tide, but he received no answer. Again Raven described the horror of children starving because there was not enough food. The giant grunted: 'I have always sat on the tide. I will always sit on the tide.' Raven spoke louder. He was getting annoyed. The giant frowned as if something was hurting his ears, but still he whispered: 'I sit on the tide.'

Then Raven knew what had to be done. He yelled: 'Get up. Stand up. Let the tide go . . . !' Still the giant did not move. Raven swept into the air and tightening his wings he let himself fall down as fast as he could. The giant jumped to his feet. As he jumped the tide which had been held since the day the world began was sucked into the gaping hole where the giant had been sitting. A great roaring sound could be heard as the waters rushed into the huge caverns.

Raven took to the air once more. He looked and looked. He could see the land which had been covered with water ever since he had first moulded the world. He flew back to the giant; settling on to his shoulders, he ordered: 'Sit down.' The giant sat down. The waters splashed and rumbled. The fish returned to the deep sea. Once more Raven flew high into the sky. He saw the ocean as it was when he had made it. The secret of the tides became known to him.

Time passed and once more Raven gazed into the giant's eyes. He heard the giant mumble: 'I am the man who sits on the tide. I have always sat on the tide.'

Raven gathered all his powers of command: 'Stand up,' he said.

'I am the man who sits on the tide,' bellowed the giant.

'Are you?' yelled Raven above the great winds. 'Are you?' He was but a speck against the darkening sky. The winds howled, but even the giant could feel the swishing sound of Raven's dive. Once more he struggled on to his feet and once more the waters sped into the cavernous depths left by his buttocks.

Raven said: 'From this time onwards you are the man who moves the tide. You sit, then you stand. Again you sit and then you stand until the end of time. Do you hear me? You are the man who moves the tide. I want human beings to catch their food with ease. I am telling you what to do.'

The giant groaned: 'I am the man who sits on the tide.' Raven sped upwards. The giant did not like the flapping sound of furious wings. He muttered to the waves: 'I am the man who moves the tide.'

Raven returned to the people of the early days. The people told him about the violent storms which had crushed their villages. They spoke of the huge floods in which many had drowned. At last they mentioned that the fish sometimes swam nearer the shore and that they were no longer hungry. Would it have to be the way of things that only dreadful storms and floods would bring them what they desperately needed? Raven's heart felt sore for his people.

Once more he travelled across the wide ocean until at last in the far distance he saw the giant's grey shape. Raven circled high in the sky watching the giant's every move. He saw the rushing haste of the waters as the giant jumped to his feet and the violent splash as the giant crashed down to the place where he had always sat.

When the ancient creature sat down Raven eased himself in front of the giant's eyes. One more the old met the old. Raven whispered to the giant words which were beyond our hearing. But when the time came for the giant to stand up, he did so gently and later at the hour of sitting down, the giant gently sank on to his buttocks.

Along the shore the people were glad as they watched how the wide waters gradually moved backwards and as they witnessed how hours later, very slowly the water came to greet their shores again. At times the fish darted in shallow waters, at times they travelled to the deep sea. When Raven landed in their midst they greeted him with glad eyes. Hunger had been banished from their land. Raven coloured the sky with delight.

2 How disease and medicine came to be

IN THE OLD DAYS the beasts, birds, fishes, insects and plants could all talk and they and the people lived together in friendship and understanding. But the people had children and their children also had children. When there were many, many people the animals lost their homes and territories. This was bad, but the animals soon found out that there was worse to come. For the people were also very clever at thinking of new ways of killing the animals. They used nets and guns and knives and traps and hooks. If you were a big animal you were hunted and slaughtered, if you were small you were poisoned or trapped underfoot. The animals knew that something had to be done. They wanted to protect themselves. What could they do?

First, the bear-tribe met in council. The Old White Bear, who was their chief, presided over the meeting. One bear after the other spoke. Each one told tales of humankind's attack on their friends and family. People flayed their skins, ate their flesh and used the bears in whatever way they liked. On hearing these tales the bears knew their anger again. They therefore decided to make war against the people.

One of them suggested that they think of a way of killing people which was similar to the way in which people killed bears. They knew this weapon only too well for was not the wood made of the trees which they loved and needed and was not the string made of the entrails of a bear, the guts of one of them? The bear-tribe therefore wanted to make one of those terrible bows in order to use it against the people who were killing them. One of the bears said that he was prepared to die so that they could make the bowstring out of his guts. They did this. They helped him to die. They also cut some wood from the locus tree to make the bow. Once the bow was ready they tried to use it. However, then they found that their claws got entangled in the bowstring. One bear offered to trim his claws. He did this. But then he could no longer climb trees. The bears were much dismayed.

Then Old White Bear spoke. He told them that this was no good. One bear had already been sacrificed, another could no longer climb trees. They had to trust their strength, their teeth and their strong claws to attack people. This was how they had been made, and this was how it had to be. They stayed together for a while longer, but no one could think of a better idea. Their war on the people did not come to much. People still don't ask the bear's pardon when they kill one. Had the bears been able to think of something better during that council, it might all have worked out different for them. As it is, bears get killed all the time.

Meanwhile the deer-tribe also met in council. Their chief was Little Deer. As they were many and as they felt kindly towards the people, they decided that a hunter was allowed to kill a deer if he first asked its pardon. Whenever this did not happen, the hunter would be struck with fierce rheumatism. For it is an offence against the deer-tribe to kill one of them without asking for pardon. The deer sent a message to the nearest Indian village, letting people know that they could only shoot a deer out of necessity. They also told the Indians how to ask the deer's pardon whenever they killed one.

When a deer has been shot by a hunter their chief Little Deer runs swiftly to the spot where the deer lies. He bends over the bloodstains and asks his dying friend if the hunter asked forgiveness. Sometimes the dying deer says 'yes', then all is well; sometimes it says 'no'. Then Little Deer follows the hunter's tracks until he finds him. This may be even to his lodge. The hunter is slain with rheumatism: he becomes crippled with pain. Most hunters know this and want to ask for pardon. Others ignore the deer's request. They build fires to cover their tracks. But Little Deer knows how to find hunters. He knows how to do this.

Some time passed and the people still killed as many animals as

they could. Then the insects, the fishes and reptiles, the birds and
the other small animals called a meeting of their tribes. The
grubworm was chosen as chief for this one council. They decided that
everyone of them should be given a chance to speak. Then they
would know whether or not people were guilty of animal slaughter,
cruelty and injustice. One after the other spoke of people's harsh
carelessness, about the pain they inflicted, about their violence.

The animals voted that they had to find a way to kill people. No
one spoke kindly about people. Only Groundsquirrel dared to say
that they had not done him much harm, and that this probably was
because he was small. The others then felt very angry and they tore
his back with their claws, which is why Groundsquirrel has stripes on
his back to this very day. The animal council remembered what the
deer-tribe had done and they too began to devise numerous diseases.
They were very clever at thinking up many diseases.

The plants had listened in silence to the animals' talk. They heard
how one disease after another was being named. Feeling friendly
towards people the plants were determined to defeat the animals' evil
designs. Each tree, shrub and herb, even the grasses and the mosses
agreed to furnish a cure for some of the diseases named. They agreed
to help people whenever their help was requested. In this way
'medicine' came to be. The plants know which diseases they can fight
but people do not always know what the plant knows. When the
medicine woman or man does not know which medicine to use for a
sick patient, the spirit of a plant suggests what is right.

3   How night appeared

I N THE OLD DAYS it was always day. There were no animals and there
was no night. At that time everything could also speak. Night was
fast asleep in the deep water.

The old people say that the daughter of the great serpent had been
given in marriage to a young man. She refused to sleep with him. The
young man thought that maybe she did not want to sleep with him
because he had three servants who were always with him. He sent his

servants away for a while. When they had gone he again asked his wife, the great serpent's daughter, to sleep with him. But she said: 'It isn't dark yet. There is only daylight. The Great Serpent who is my father has the night. Fetch the darkness from the river. Then you may sleep with me.'

The young man asked that his servants return. They listened to the daughter of the Great Serpent. She told them to travel to her father's dwelling and say that she had sent them to fetch the tucuma nut.

They came to the Great Serpent's dwelling and were given the tucuma nut. It was completely sealed. When the Great Serpent, the daughter's father, handed them the nut, he said: 'Do not open the nut. You must not open the nut. It will not be good if you open the nut.' They could hear that there was a sound inside the nut. It was a strange *ti-ti-ti* sound. Now we know that it is the sound of crickets and frogs and toads. They sing during the night. At that time, however, there were no animals and there was no night and the servants did not recognise the sound.

The three servants went on their way. They paddled as fast as they could for the *ti-ti-ti* sound had not stopped and they so much wanted to open the nut. They wanted to open it. They thought that if they paddled fast, they might not succumb. Had not the Great Serpent told them that it would not be good if they opened the nut? They did not do it. They kept paddling as fast as they could. They had gone a long way when they rested their paddles in the middle of the river.

They made a fire in the canoe. they opened the tucuma nut and the first night rushed out of the nut. It was very dark. It was dark everywhere. Now the daughter of the Great Serpent would know that they had opened the nut. They were frightened and continued their journey home.

In that place the young woman said to her husband that his servants had opened the nut and now they must wait for dawn. This was the first dawn. It happened when the first dawn arrived, the many things in the forest became birds and animals. They became animals and birds when dawn broke. Ducks and fishes were born from what had been drifting about in the river. The jaguar came from a basket.

Then the morning star appeared. When the daughter of the Great Serpent saw the morning star she decided to make a separation between day and night. She spun a thread, rolled it between her fingers and moulded a cujubi-bird. Its head was made white with some white clay and the legs were made red with urucu, the red dye. She spoke to the cujubi-bird and said: 'When dawn comes, you will sing.' She spun another thread, rolled it between her fingers and moulded an inambu-bird. She also made some ashes. She rubbed the ashes on the bird's body, saying: 'You are the inambu-bird. You will sing many times during the night.' Since that time birds do call during the night; and as soon as morning breaks, they tell people about the night's journey.

The three servants returned to the home of the Great Serpent's daughter. Here they were punished by the young man for they had not done as they had been told. They were the ones who had opened the tucuma nut. Because the servants opened the tucuma nut all the things which had been in the forest, and those which had been adrift on the water, were for ever changed. The young man therefore made his three servants into monkeys. They live in trees.

4 The king and the oak

A LONG TIME AGO in Thessaly there was a beautiful grove. Here trees grew undisturbed. Wild bees made their honey. Birds sang in gently swaying tree-tops and little fawns rested in the shade. It was a safe and glorious place. In the middle of an open glade there stood a mighty oak. Near the oak were fountains. They were the most sparkling fountains anyone had ever seen. In that distant grove every tree and every bush was fresh and green.

Once in a while people visited the valley. They entered the wood in dreamy trepidation for they knew that the great goddess Ceres had her temple in the glade of the oak. The trees near the entrance of the grove changed the purposeful traveller's urgency into a willing surrender to the lush valley's slow, steady pace. Thus all was peaceful in that vale. Here the fruit of the earth was loved and Ceres, the great goddess, listened to the people who came to beg her help. Near the base of the great oak were many small gifts, lingering witnesses to the grace bestowed by Ceres.

In every tree there lived a hamadryad or wood-nymph. The tree's life and the wood-nymph's life were interwoven. Whenever a tree died, the wood-nymph died. Therefore the wood in the grove was never cut. Each tree grew until it had reached the fullness of its years, or until thunder or great storms brought an early end to the life of the tree which reaches upward into the sky.

Near the valley of Ceres there lived a king. He was mighty and prosperous, which is dangerous for kings. In order to show the world his wealth as well as his power he decided to build a new palace. He designed it himself. It had to be higher and wider than any palace he had ever visited. Of course he would need the tallest and oldest trees in the country to create the largest roof ever made, a roof which had

to span the majestic width of his new palace. He knew where such trees grew. Not hesitating for a moment he instructed twenty woodcutters to take their best axes and follow him to the sacred grove.

When the king entered the grove he did not see the gnawing darkness which fell upon the ancient forest nor did he hear the warning in the rustle of the trees. The woodcutters trembled before the grove's sacredness, but the king shouted angrily and told them to cut down every tree in sight, to cast their axe deep into the trees' strong body.

The men could not lift their axes. They could not will themselves to do as they had been told. Because the woodcutters failed to savage the trees he so desired, the king's rage grew. He ran deeper and deeper into the grove. The woodcutters followed; loneliness ravaged their faces. Then in great fury the king tore a big axe towards himself. He lifted it and with one blind stroke he cut the blade far into the great oak's trunk. A piercing cry ran through the skies. It was the wounded cry of the hamadryad, the wood-nymph. He told himself that the axe was singing a triumphant song. Thus he ignored the wood-nymph's burst of grievous pain. Again he hacked wildly into the tree.

At that moment an old priestess came from the temple which stood near the great oak. She approached the king saying that he was unwise to anger the great goddess Ceres. Was she not the power of growth in everything that flourishes on earth? But the king, he did not listen. He spat insults at the old priestess. This oak had to be cut apart. He wanted it to support his palace roof.

The old priestess urged him once more to be careful. He did not listen. Then she walked away and the woodcutters saw that her face was the face of Ceres.

The great oak fell. The wood-nymph died. Her last moan added to the darkness. The other wood-nymphs in the valley answered her dying wail. The woodcutters were very frightened. They wanted to leave the valley, but they did not do so. Instead they obeyed their king, felling every single tree.

It was not long before the king's new palace was finished and it was majestic indeed. The king knew that he had insulted the great goddess, but as nothing unusual had happened during the building of the palace, he soon comforted himself. Her powers must be limited. Not even Ceres could punish him.

Then, at Ceres' command, hunger came to Thessaly. Hunger was one of Ceres' trusted servants. She had the power to stunt growth. Wherever she went, she sowed her barren seed. No longer did the fountains bubble towards the sky. Rivers ceased their flow. Hunger also prevented the rain from falling. The peasants who dwelled in the once lush hills took their remaining livestock and followed the trail of sorrowful hope which led to other lands. They searched for a new home and found it.

Soon Hunger entered the king's own palace sowing strife and fury amongst his servants. They abandoned the king. At last only the king and his daughter Metra lived in the palace. She stayed loyally by his side. Travellers who still passed through the king's country invariably carried ample supplies of food and water. The king and his daughter raised their hands towards these strangers, exchanging their precious objects for food. Sometimes they begged. When there were no other precious objects left, the king sold his daughter to a passing merchant. She became a slave. The food thus gained did not last long. Then the king died.

The sacred grove remained for ever barren. The wood-nymphs did not return. Though Ceres did punish the king, she could not make the valley lush again. Not even Ceres can do this.

5   Dream dilemma

A LONG TIME AGO a man called Chuang Tzu had a dream. It was a beautiful dream. In his dream he was a butterfly. A butterfly who could follow his heart's desire without galling constraint: gently adrift on the air, then winging his way to a flower with clear, open petals.

Chuang Tzu woke up and touched his skin. He felt more than a little frightened. Was he Chuang Tzu, a man who dreamt that he was a very happy butterfly or was he a butterfly who happened to dream that he was Chuang Tzu?

Was there any real difference between Chuang-Tzu and the butterfly?

6 *Mouse wants her tail back*

THE CAT and the mouse
Play'd in the malt-house:

The cat snatched the mouse's tail. She bit right through it.
'Pray, pussycat give me my tail again.'
'I won't give you your tail,' says the cat, 'until you fetch me some milk. Fetch it from the cow.'

First Mouse leapt, and then Mouse ran,
Till she came to the cow, and thus began:

'Pray, Cow, give me your milk. I'll give the milk to the cat and the cat will give me my tail again.'
'I won't give you milk,' says the cow. 'Go fetch me some hay. Fetch it from the farmer.'

First Mouse leapt, and then Mouse ran,
Till she came to the farmer, and thus began:

'Pray, Farmer, give me some hay. Then I'll give hay to the cow, who will give me some milk, I'll give the milk to the cat, who will give me my tail again.'
'I won't give you hay,' says the farmer. 'Go to the butcher and fetch me some meat.'

First Mouse leapt, and then Mouse ran,
Till she came to the butcher, and thus began:

'Pray, Butcher, give me some meat. I'll give the meat to the farmer, who'll give me hay for the cow, the cow will give me milk which I'll give to the cat and the cat will give me my tail again.'
'Oh, no,' says the butcher. 'Go to the baker and fetch me some bread.'

First Mouse leapt, and then Mouse ran,
Till she came to the baker, and thus began:

'Pray, Baker, give me some bread. I'll give it to the butcher, who'll give me meat, which I'll give to the farmer, who'll give me hay, which goes to the cow, who will give me milk, which I'll give to the cat, who will give me my tail again.'

'Yes I will,' said the baker. 'I will give you bread,
But don't you dare eat my meal or I'll cut off your head.'

Then the baker gave the mouse bread, and Mouse gave the butcher bread, Butcher gave the mouse meat, Mouse gave the farmer meat, Farmer gave the mouse hay, Mouse gave the cow hay, Cow gave the mouse milk and Mouse gave the cat milk and Cat gave Mouse her very own tail again.

Working with the stories

Raven and the man who sat on the tide
WHEN CHANGE MATTERS

Use a drum. Whilst drum is beaten in a steady rhythm, move quickly through the room. Faster and faster. As soon as drumbeat stops – *freeze*. When drumbeat starts again – move. Repeat, freezing in different positions.

Return to circle.

Tell the story 'Raven and the Man who sat on the Tide'.

Reflect on situations in your life which are evoked by this story. It does not matter if at the moment you do not quite understand the links.

Mention these situations without going into detail, e.g. rows between my parents, when I borrowed my friend's gardening tools, a scene I witnessed in the post office.

Talk in groups of three or four for ten minutes about the scenes in greater detail.

Select one of the scenes and create a mini-drama. Rehearse your work.

Present your dramatisations to the other groups.

Discuss the dramas you've just seen. Especially any underlying themes related to willingness or refusal to change. Make connections too with the story.

Return to your small group.

Talk about the work you did together. Anything you learned?

Return to the circle and reflect upon the entire session.

How disease and medicine came to be
POWERLESSNESS AND EMPOWERMENT

Decide what kind of forest animal you want to be at a later point during the session.

Write on one side of a sheet of paper the word *health*; on the other side, the word *sickness*.

List quickly all the associated words which come to mind.

Paint two separate images on a sheet of paper: your image of sickness and your image of health.

Write anything else you wish to record.

Talk a little about your paintings.

Tell the story 'How Disease and Medicine Came to Be'. Remind yourself of the forest animal you wanted to be. A long time has passed since the animal councils met. Your animal knows about the impact of sickness and health on people. It also knows about people's treatment of animals. Your animal therefore decides to write a letter both to people and to the other animals.

Write this letter.

Create a performance area. Place a chair in this space. The chair is used to read the animal's letter to the people and other animals.

Read the letters.

RESPONSE TASK: discuss your response to the letters in groups of three or four. Focus on the feelings evoked and then ask yourselves what needs to be changed/done in order to bring about betterment.

Return to the circle.

Share your ideas.

Reflect upon the entire session.

How night appeared

THE TWILIGHT HOURS

Imagine that you are in a strange environment. You are sitting quite still. Suddenly you hear unusual noises. Together the group will create these sounds. If it feels all right, please close your eyes. Join in with the sounds when you feel ready to do so.

Create the sound-scene.

Talk a little with the people on your left and right about the images evoked by the sounds.

Remind yourself of a beautiful sunrise/sunset.

Join a group of three or four.

Share your memories. Then decide whether your group will work around the theme of sunrise or sunset.

Work together to create a brief movement improvisation around your theme. Your work will start more easily if you stand up and adopt a starting posture expressive of the emotion evoked in you when you realise(d) that the sun is about to rise/set.

Present your work to the other group members.

Talk a little about the presentations and the feelings/memories they evoked.

Tell the story 'How Night Appeared'.

Work together to create a group painting to represent those aspects of the story which the group considers important. Talk for a few minutes to bring these aspects to the fore, then begin the painting. Encourage the group to use finger-paints.

When the painting is finished, talk about the work and especially about the way in which the group interacted during the painting. Make connections with the feelings evoked by the images of sunrise and sunset. Note: some group members may feel quite melancholic/angry, and have difficulty with the cycle of light and darkness.

Select any themes which may need to be remembered and returned to during later sessions.

RESPONSE TASK: imagine that you hold snugly in the palm of your hands, a heart-warming gift, which you intend to give away to other group members. You have as many of these gifts as you desire to give away. You can receive as many as come your way. Give/receive these gifts.

Close the session.

The king and the oak

TREES IN TROUBLE

Remember a tree which has been or is important to you.

Briefly share the history of your relationship with this tree with the group.

RESPONSE TASK: on a sheet of paper create as many spaces as there are group members. After each person has told their memory, make a small drawing of their tree in one of the spaces.

Reflect a while on your tree drawings.

Tell the story 'The King and the Oak'.

Distribute copies of the text.

Read the story quietly by yourself.

Join a group of three or four people.

Decide which three scenes you consider to be the most important ones in this tale. Once you've reached agreement, create a *tableau vivant* of this scene. Make sure every person in your small group has a role in these group sculptures.

Present your 'sculpted' scenes.

Discuss the scenes, their similarities and differences. Note also which aspects of the story have not been represented in the group sculptures.

Look at your earlier tree drawing.

Choose a partner.

RESPONSE TASK: discuss with a partner which feelings have been evoked in you. Explore which active contribution you can make to protect/plant trees.

Share these thoughts with the group.

Reflect upon the entire session.

Dream dilemma

BEYOND DREAMY INDOLENCE

Stand in a circle. Shoulders relaxed. Knees slightly bent. Breathe out. Allow breathing to develop from breathing out. Notice how your breath changes as you breathe out. Do this a few times.

In pairs sitting opposite each other, make eye contact. Decide who will begin the exercise. Each has three minutes. One person speaks a sentence beginning with 'I . . .'. The other person repeats the sentence, starting with 'You . . .'. E.g. A: 'I live alone.' B: 'You live alone.' Or A: 'I have not been on holiday for a while.' B: 'You have not been on holiday for a while.'

After three minutes – change roles.

Discuss the experience.

Return to the circle.

Talk a little about the experience you have just had.

Write on one large sheet of paper as many feeling words as the group can think up: e.g. happy, confused, mad, bored.

Join a group of three or four people. Select three or four feeling words which your group wants to explore.

Explore these words using movement only. The exploration is made easier if you all stand up, adopt a posture which to you expresses these words, and then interact with each other using sound and movement only.

Give a copy of the story to each small group.

Read the story 'Dream Dilemma'.

Imagine a scene which happened the night before this man had the dream. A scene which may have contributed to the dreaming. Also think of a scene which might happen the morning after he dreamt the dream. Allow your imagination to be inspired by the feeling words.

Rehearse these scenes. Take care that each scene involves every person in your small group.

Present your scenes to one another.

Return to your small group and discuss the experience.

RESPONSE TASK: return to the first person with whom you worked during this session. Remind yourselves of the 'I am . . . ' statements. Discuss one situation in your life where it would be helpful if you could be more assertive. Think of the feeling you need to draw on in order to achieve this. Share this with your partner.

Return to the circle.

Share any thoughts/reflections evoked.

Closure Repeat the breathing exercise.

Mouse wants her tail back

ALWAYS THE WEAKEST?

Play 'Fox and lambs'. (You will need one small cushion or soft ball). One group member is the fox, the others are lambs. The fox tries to capture lambs by placing the cushion against their chest. This can be avoided by standing chest-to-chest with another lamb, but this can only last for a count of three. Then the lambs must once more be on the move.

List many different situations in which a personal choice has to be made, e.g. where to go on holiday; whether or not to lend money to a friend; whether or not to reveal that you've lied.

In pairs develop a dramatic scene leading up to a moment of choice. Stop just before the choice has to be made.

Present your scenes.

Discuss the scenes.

Give a copy of 'Mouse Wants her Tail Back' to every group member.

Read the story. Then re-read it and imagine that this is the coded text of a tragedy. What is the tragedy? Each person writes their real story for which this one is the cover-up.

Read the 'text-beneath-the-text' stories.

RESPONSE TASK: Create as many small pieces of paper as there are group members. Whenever a group member has finished their story think of some words of advice which you have for one of the characters in their story: e.g. for the young girl: 'Respect must be earned as well as granted'.

Give the pieces of advice to the group members concerned.

Read what you have received.

Select one or two which feel pertinent to you.

Share these with the group.

Reflect on the entire session.

A few questions to explore

○ What causes the tides?

○ Which types of seashore do you know?

o What are the advantages and disadvantages of modern commercial fishing? Which methods are used?

o How are waves caused?

o What are the proportions of land and sea in relation to the earth's surface?

o Why are the rocks in the oceanic crust younger than those of the continents?

o What kind of adaptations to life on the seashore need to be made by plants, animals and people?

o What is meant by 'disease'. How is it possible for disease to develop in healthy organisms?

o What do bears use their claws for?

o How do plants live? Why are they so very important?

o What are medicines? Why are plants often used as the basis for medicines?

o What are the differences between night and day?

o What happens during the night?

o Why are apes and monkeys called intelligent creatures?

o What are the differences between vertebrate and invertebrate animals?

o Why do so many invertebrate animals live hidden from view?

o What are the main temperate hardwood trees? Why have they mostly disappeared from our landscape?

o What happens to land once the trees have been felled?

o What are dreams?

o Why do people and some animals dream?

o What is the process of development of a butterfly?

o What are the functions of animals' tails?

THREE

A LONG WAY FROM HOME

I neither thought the sun,
Nor moon, nor stars, nor people, mine,
Tho' they did round about me shine;
And therefore was I quite undone.
THOMAS TRAHERNE

A solution to the knot, which the group itself constructed, is found. It must be found if the group wants to survive. Retrospectively we could have predicted the period of doubt after the initial enthusiasm. After all it was untested, and as such both innocent and unrealistic. Once this is recognised the entire group process can ease up and further shared experiences soon give reason for the continuation of the enterprise, even though at this stage some people may actually leave the group because it is not right for them. Their departure is then inspired by a choice between priorities and not because difference within the group feels too uncomfortable. Hopefully such departure is preceded by some discussion of the reasons for leaving and an acknowledgement of the gains derived from the brief period of interaction.

Having been slightly reduced in size the group is left with a core of people who genuinely intend to work together. Obviously the aims need to be adjusted. The renewed commitment to the task in hand is likely to result in a fruitful period of work which lasts several sessions. But then once more we encounter a vying for power and leadership. This time more obviously so. This tends to cause irritation and is best dealt with by exploring the roles which people play within the group. To clarify the spheres of influence. The group then needs to pay some attention to the various ways in which members identify with one another; to discover also how vulnerabilities contribute to the group's overall strength. Actual support is needed.

At times it will seem as if suddenly the focus of attention is on internal process, not on achieving external results. Will no one hear how important the project is? It is, but maybe it is more important at this stage of the journey to emphasise the existence of mutual care. We will probably have some trouble seeing what can be done to improve the situation in the here and now of the group. It appears to have got stuck again and to suffer from multiple ignorance syndrome. Yet any attempt to lift the veil of unknowing is responded to with either fear or outrage. Vulnerable to contradictory realities, other people's perceptions are denied validity. There is a rigid clinging to one's own interpretation of felt reality, whilst privately everyone thinks that the required change of attitudes and actions cannot be delivered: 'We do not have it in us.' We wonder whether or not to leave the group because we feel not up to the group's high standards and expectations, yet unable to mention our insecurity. Consequently the felt sense of pretence is getting us down. It becomes a somewhat acute disturbance.

The earlier experiences with other groups offer us a context for what is happening. This is not necessarily helpful as some of those groups are likely to have collapsed at this stage. To set a benign circle of change into motion is never easy. It is even more difficult to maintain it. Because the relationships between group members have been sustained for a while, the expectations are growing. The work which the group continues to undertake on immediate issues does provide a developing sense of confidence in members' actual abilities. This is in seeming contradiction to the enhanced internal tensions. However, both processes tend to go hand in hand. The first steps towards actual change are being taken, but we ourselves are the last ones to know it. Occasionally someone mentions that 'things' are changing.

There is a gradually emerging sense that the group is learning to weather storms and equally that further adaptive changes will be required. Maybe that in change processes our capacity for self-repair matters more than we had presumed. Once this is realised a spirit of optimism slowly enters the group. It is proposed that we only have to re-clarify our goals. That's all . . . ?!

The goals have to be reformulated because the group is now actually working and weaknesses in the frame of reference are likely to have been revealed. This troubles some members. During this period of re-evaluation of goals the occasional bout of fatalism is harder to contain. At times this leads to conflict within the group. Our trust in each other, and in our perceptions of the situation, is and must be tested. There are accusations of dishonesty, of manipulation too. Whereas during the earlier stages of group-development members competed with each other for leadership, now there appears to be a blatant competition for followers, the attempt to recruit supporters for alternative causes and goals.

The group is in actual danger of being split. Discussions about the advisability of such a division are likely to occur. It is said that maybe people should go their different ways, each section pursuing alternative paths towards similar aims. How to contain multi-variousness without bitterness and resentment? It is obviously difficult to tolerate ambiguity or alternatives. The longing 'to get it right' rears its powerful head. Once this is recognised, we learn what contributes to our investment in perfection. This tends to be a sorrowful stage. It hurts. The previous actions and omissions need to be mourned. Mourning slows the group down, but it also brings the members closer together. We become more dependant on each other. Dependancy which causes its own panic. However, we have learned to recognise the signs of fear and consequently can offer each other some containment. More so than during the early stages of group formation. The loss of innocent expectation, which we did not even know we had, is hard. Greater tolerance and gentleness towards each other are the gains. We need such gains for the next stages of our journey.

1 Riverturtle is not singing

ONCE UPON A TIME a little Riverturtle was travelling along very slowly. Turtles cannot go fast at the best of times, but this was a particularly warm day and the little turtle had trudged a long way from home. The ground had still been covered with dew when he left the river where he lived. Somehow he had not noticed that he was going further and further away from the river on to the dry rocky land. He forgot that riverturtles must always stay damp. It is dangerous for them to dry out. When their shell is dry they get tired and when the sun shines upon their shell for hours on end, they may even die. Our little turtle did not think of any of these things as he meandered past small stones that looked like high mountains. Sauntering happily as if nothing bad could ever happen to him.

Now, in this place there weren't any trees or bushes, just rocks and sand. Suddenly little Riverturtle felt that the sun had been shining on his back for a long, long time. He felt so hot. Where was he? He looked round. For the first time since he had been on his great journey he looked around and he knew: he was a long way from home. He hastened back to the river, but the heat was torrid and little Riverturtle could not go any further. At last he saw a shady hole in a big rock. He dragged himself towards it and climbed into the hole.

As soon as he was safe inside the hole, he began to cry. Great big turtletears fell on to this feet. He could feel them drip down his cheeks. This made him cry even louder. He cried so hard that Mr Coyote, who was walking by, heard the sound. Mr Coyote stopped and cocked his ears. Someone was singing. He knew it. Someone was singing a beautiful song. How he loved that song. He had to learn it. Therefore Mr Coyote followed his ears. Soon he found the hole beneath the rock where little Riverturtle cried his big frightened tears.

'Good afternoon to you,' said Mr Coyote. 'You are singing a powerful song. I so much want to learn it. Could you please teach me?' Little turtle was startled to see Mr Coyote – and anyhow he was crying, not singing. How could anyone think that he was singing when he was so afraid and a long way from home? Mr Coyote asked again: 'Can you teach me that song?'

'I did not sing a song,' said little Riverturtle.

'Don't lie to me,' said Mr Coyote, 'Don't deceive me. I know you were singing and I want to learn that song. If you don't teach me the song, that'll be the end of you.'

Then little Riverturtle knew who he was dealing with and he said: 'You don't know what's coming if you try to eat me. My shell will stick in your throat and make you choke. You'll never sing.'

'I want to learn that song,' said Mr Coyote. 'That's what I want. I shall throw you out into the sun if you don't teach me. That's what I'll do.'

'So what?' said little Riverturtle defiantly: 'That won't hurt me. I'll creep into my shell. So what if you throw me into the sun?'

Mr Coyote got very angry with little Riverturtle. He said: 'Well, in that case I will throw you into the river. You must sing for me.'

Then little Riverturtle pleaded: 'Mr Coyote, please don't throw me into the river. Not the river. I shall drown. I'll die. I'll never sing again. Not into the river, please, Mr Coyote.'

'Oh yes, I will,' said Mr Coyote. He grabbed little Riverturtle between his teeth, ran as fast as he could and threw him into the river.

Little Riverturtle swam away as fast as he could. Then he popped his head above the water and said sweetly: 'Thank you Mr Coyote. Thank you for helping me.'

Mr Coyote, he ambled away. He never learned the song.

2   Crow and Frog

CROW CAUGHT a lovely, succulent frog. She clasped Frog in her bill and hastily flew to the roof of a house which was not far from the place where she had been lucky enough to catch her prey. It gave Crow much pleasure that she would be able to eat her food in peace and quiet. When she settled down on the roof she was greatly surprised to hear laughter. It was only a little laugh, but Frog laughed.

'Why are you laughing, Sister Frog?' Crow asked. She was after all about to devour her.

'Nothing much,' said Frog, 'It's just . . . Oh, don't worry . . . It's just that it so happens that my mother lives on this very roof. She is unbelievably strong and she'll be so angry when she sees that you're trying to eat me or even to hurt me.' Frog laughed again.

Crow did not like the sound of it. She snapped Frog tightly into her bill and hopped off to the part of the roof where the rainwater falls down a little hole. She settled down again and made ready to eat her food. Then Frog giggled.

'Why are you giggling, Sister Frog?' Crow enquired.

'Oh Sister, truly, I don't want to bother you. It really is nothing very much. Only . . . ' said Frog merrily: 'You took me here because of my mother, and now we're near my uncle. He is my mother's elder brother. He is strong and loves me dearly. If he knew that you were trying to injure me . . . '

Waggish Frog smiled at Sister Crow, who was more than a little alarmed. She took Frog in her bill and flew to the ground below. She landed by the side of a well. What else could she have done?

She had only just opened her beak to start eating Frog when she heard Frog say: 'Oh, Sister Crow, as you were picking me up and putting me down, I noticed that your bill is not very sharp. In fact, it is rather blunt. It would be nice if you could just sharpen it a little before you eat me. You could use that stone over there.'

Crow liked the thought of eating with a sharp bill. It is so much easier to eat a frog when your beak has just been stropped. She hopped to the stone and proceeded to sharpen her bill.

Meanwhile Frog jumped into the well. What else could she have done?

Then, ready to eat, Crow returned to look for Frog. She did not see Frog where she had left her. Where had she gone? Maybe she had gone into the well. Crow hopped on to the little wall which surrounded the well. She craned her head from side to side. Yes, there was Sister Frog. 'Oh, Sister Frog,' she cried: 'I was so worried I had lost you. My bill is quite nice and sharp now. So please come along up and be eaten.'

Frog chuckled. The very same chuckle Crow had heard on the roof. Then she heard Frog say: 'The well is too deep, Sister Crow, I cannot get up these walls. Why don't you come down and meet me here at the bottom of the well?'

Sister Crow did not see Frog again.

3 *The evil bet*

T HE DAY PORTENDED EVIL. Two men made a bet and thereby cast a
sombre lot over the sultan's city. They boasted that their power
was great, which led them to wondering which one of them could
destroy the city more rapidly than the other. They were: the liar and
the sorcerer.

First the sorcerer came to the innocent town. Innocent to the
battle which the two men had started in earnest. The sorcerer killed
fifty people, using strong poison and other magical tricks. That is all
he did. When relatives and friends suddenly died the city dwellers
were terrified, but when nothing more happened, they mourned
their losses. They could not understand the mysterious deaths.
However, because one day followed the next, they stopped wondering and life continued as before.

When he saw that the people went about their business as usual, the sorcerer departed from the sultan's city. He said to the liar: 'I may have lost our wager. You try.'

The liar went to the city. He hastened to the sultan's palace. It was not long before he was one of the sultan's favourite advisers. The day came when he whispered into the sultan's ear: 'You need to know that your brother Salimu is raising an army against you. As you know my sources are always reliable.'

'I am not surprised,' said the sultan. 'He is a terrible man.'

The liar left the sultan's palace and touched the citizens with the rumour that war was imminent. 'Prepare yourself,' he said, 'Prepare.'

The people bought swords and guns and powder. They made ready for war. Soon both brothers noticed the will to war. The enemy lived within their gates. Two armies were called to the trigger. The sultan struck first. Salimu fought back. He won the battle and the sultan's city was destroyed.

The liar and the sorcerer met at the appointed hour. The liar smiled triumphantly saying: 'There is no need for poison and magical spells. They are too slow. You saw that it was easy. People do not need much help to destroy each other on our behalf. You must let them do it for you.'

The sorcerer looked away. He thought: 'This man is evil.'

Know the liar.

4   The fishpond of Paaiea

MANY YEARS AGO only the most skilled fishermen dared to paddle their boats past Ka-Lae-O-Keahole, the western cape of the island of Hawaii, where tide, current and wind conspired to create fierce waves. Some fishermen so dreaded the cape that they would steer their canoes into a large fishpond which lay just before the cape's extreme, taking their catch to shore in the safety of the pond's sheltered waters. Before too long every sensible fisherman in the district did the same. The strong southerly sea breeze dictated the will of the waves and the fishermen adjusted accordingly.

At that time the fishpond belonged to a certain chief. He was a greedy man who decreed that it was forbidden to eat fish on the pond's shore. Neither were people allowed to carry their fish home until the chief's overseer, Kepaalani granted them permission to do so. The overseer had many helpers who guarded the place with great ferocity and in this case too the fishermen submitted to the seemingly inevitable rules.

One day an old woman paddled her canoe into the bay. On the shore near Kepaalani's shed a group of fishermen were gutting a large catch of bonito. Soon the fish would be ready for drying. The old woman saw that the canoes were still full of fish which had to be carried ashore. It was the bonito season and the ocean had granted the fishermen a rich offering.

Having decorated herself with a wreath of beautiful yellow flowers, the old woman was a pleasure to behold. The fishermen could smell the flowers' sweet scent even as they gutted yet another bonito. When the people looked at the strange old lady, they said 'Aloha' and she replied 'Aloha'.

Then a man by the name of Kapulau approached her saying, 'Malihini?' (which means: 'Are you a stranger?').

She smiled and said, 'I dwell in this place and belong here. However, I rarely visit the ocean shore. Because I live where the mountains are wild I do not often eat fish. Knowing that the season is plentiful I have come to ask for some fish-innards.'

Kapulau answered: 'Indeed we do have fish and fish-innards in abundance, but in this place Kepaalani is the only one who can give you permission to eat fish or to take some away. The chief gave him that power. He sits right there. Do go and ask him for what you want.'

The old woman went on her way. Kapulau followed her with his gaze. He saw that a large group of people trailed behind her. He rubbed his eyes. She had arrived in one canoe. Who were these people?

The old woman approached Kepaalani. He too greeted her, saying, 'A stranger? Where have you come from.'

She replied: 'From the place where the land is wild and unapproachable. I heard that the sea has granted you a generous catch. I have come to ask for some fish.'

The chief had taken care to appoint the right overseer: 'No fish,' Kepaalani replied sternly. 'Only the men who serve the chief are given fish. I made this decision on the chief's behalf. That is what I have decided. Only the chief's men are given fish.'

The woman changed tack. 'Well. Maybe you cannot give me fish, but what about some fish-innards?'

'Only the men who serve the chief are given fish-innards.'

'But can you not give me just a few shrimps from the fishpond?' she still tried.

'Old woman, I have told you. You will not be given fish or fish-innards or shrimps. None of these will be given to you. Every single one belongs to the chief and to the chief only. He decided it that way. I am doing as I am told. He is the only one who could give you what you ask for.'

'Enough . . . I have heard enough,' said the old woman. 'I shall return to my home where the land is wild and unapproachable. I shall not even take a grain of salt.' She turned around and went. The fishermen who witnessed her going saw the large crowd of people who walked behind her. They left the shore.

Halfway up the mountain the old woman came to Kapulau's dwelling. When he had been unable to honour her humble request for some fish-innards, Kapulau had hurried home. When she approached his dwellingplace, he pleaded with her to enter and eat some fish. It was a generous offering. She ate and when she made ready to go, Kapulau offered her more fish for the journey home.

Before turning away to walk to the place where the land is wild and unapproachable, she said to him: 'When night has fallen, bind this cloth to the back and the front of your house. Those who have ears have heard it said that this will be a great and restless night. Protect yourself and you will be safe. No harm will come to you.' She started to climb the mountain. Though the trail was visible the woman mysteriously disappeared from sight. Kapulau looked for her appearance round the next twist of the mountain path. She was not there.

Night came. The mountains of Hualalai burst into fire and glowing lava ran down the slopes of the land which is wild and unapproachable. The old woman's simple request for fish or fish-innards or even shrimps had been refused. She was no other than

Pele, the goddess of the volcano. Great streams of lava entered the
fish-pond of Paaiea. Now there are black rocks where once the people
caught fish in abundance.

The lava never reached Kapulaiu's house. It did not even touch his
gates.

5 When Emu and Wild Turkey inflicted grief

I N THE DREAMTIME there were two sisters: Wildura, the wild turkey,
and Waraji, the emu. Both were the proud mothers of a large
family of chicks. Their pride led them to comparing their offspring
with each other. Emu did not like these comparisons for she was the
younger sister and always felt inferior. She knew that being the
younger one gave her less social importance and even though her
chicks were quite as beautiful and talented as her sister's she always
showed them off and praised their qualities by putting Wild Turkey's
children down.

She tried to make her sister's heart sore by putting her children
down, but it was of little use, for her elder sister's children were lovely.
Thus Emu became more and more jealous. She helplessly surrendered
to her envy that she was not the firstborn. Being secondborn she felt
that she could never be the best in anything, nor could her children.
Would she just have to accept that this was the way it had to be?

Emu tried to forget about the issue, but she minded very much.
She always felt the loser. Even though Wild Turkey denied that there
was even a contest. She would, for she always won. Then Emu had a
thought. She was very pleased with herself. If she could think of a
clever way by which Wild Turkey would kill some of her own
children, she would be the one who had the largest family. This
would make her a more important creature than Wild Turkey. Of
course it would. She should have thought of this before. It was very
simple.

The birds and animals had been on their daily round of food
gathering. Emu had not joined them. This was unusual. When she

came back that evening, she folded her wings over all but two of her chicks. Wild Turkey who was anxious about her sister's absence, approached her. She could only see two chicks and asked where the others were. Emu replied casually:

'Oh, I have killed them. They weren't worth the bother. It was so much work. Now I have only got two chicks to look after. They will grow into strong, large birds. I wonder why you don't kill yours too.'

Wild Turkey was not enamoured with her sister's advice. Killing her chicks was not something she was ready to do. But as time passed by, she grew very tired of feeding her large demanding family. Meanwhile her sister battered Wild Turkey with arguments, saying that she was foolish not to try killing her chicks. It was very easy. Emu persuaded her older sister. Wild Turkey gave in. With a heavy heart she killed all but two of her chicks.

Then Emu opened her wings. There they were. All her chicks were alive and well. Wild Turkey realised that she had been sorely tricked. She went to see her husband and told him the whole story. Together they sorrowed for many days. Then grief made way for rage. Rage inspired revenge.

They waited, the wild turkey and her husband, and carefully laid their plans. They taught themselves how to tuck their wings close into their bodies. Anyone looking at them would have thought that their wings had been cut.

On a particularly hot day they walked towards Emu's camp announcing with great joy that they had something marvellous. They had cut their wings. They were now so cool. It was unbelievably comfortable. They also looked thinner and more elegant. Emu's jealousy rose to her throat. She could not bear it. They had killed their own chicks and now they stood before her, laughing and dancing about gleefully, saying that they were happy and praising each other's beauty.

Emu took a sharp stone and cut her wings too. Then the Wild Turkeys shrieked with delight. They opened their wings and circled about. 'You will be chased by people and dogs. You'll get killed.'

They spat their words at her. Then they flew away.

6 *The animals argue about the length of day and night*

I N THAT TIME there were many animal people. There was no night. There was no day. The animal people asked each other whether they must name night and day. They talked until they quarrelled. They quarrelled about naming night and day. They did not agree. Grizzly was there, Cougar, Wolf, Badger, Coyote, Fisher and all the others. They had come together to talk about this and found many voices. They wondered how long the night should be. Should there be only one day and then one night of darkness?

Bear spoke and decreed that there should be five days and one darkness. That's how he wanted it. Dawn would come on the fifth day. Bear's older brother Grizzly said that this was not good. Ten years he wanted. 'Ten years of light and then one darkness.' Those were Grizzly's words. Rattlesnake thought otherwise. He wanted five years. Rattlesnake's younger brother, the one who is called Bull-snake, whispered that he wanted three years and then one dawn. These were the thoughts of the Bears and Grizzly's and Snakes.

All the animal people were at this gathering. Each found a voice. The Toad people certainly did not want it to be like this, the way of the Bear people and the Snake people. They did not want so many years to pass and then one darkness, for the people (the Indians) would soon be there. Never could it be this way. They wanted one day and one night only. This was how Toad spoke. All the animal people argued. Then Frog, who is Toad's younger brother, opened his voice. He said: 'Let there be only one day and only one night. One night and then dawn shall come.'

Grizzly was angry. The animal people feared his anger, for he was powerful in their land and dangerous. Rattlesnake was also dangerous. They feared Rattlesnake too. Bear and Rattler were angry. They did not want it that way. They were very angry. The animal people, those gathered in that place, said: 'We will argue about it. When darkness falls, we will argue. The one who has the strength to talk till dawn will win. That is how we want it. Soon the people (the

Indians) shall be with us. Day for ten years can never be. Day for five years cannot be. Day for three years cannot be.' This is how they spoke.

They did speak when darkness came. Grizzly said: 'Ten years, one darkness.' Frog argued: 'Only one day, only one night.' Grizzly insisted: 'Ten years, one darkness.' 'One day, one night,' Frog said.

When dawn came Grizzly was very tired. Frog did win. When the sun rose Frog said again: 'One day, one night. Only one night.' This is how Frog beat Grizzly. They argued in this manner. Since that time there is only one day and only one darkness. Then there is dawn.

Working with the stories

Riverturtle is not singing

BEYOND FEELING LOST

Stretch up and right through, without raising shoulders. And again and again. Yawn at the end of each stretch.

Shake every part of your body. Begin with your hands and wrists. Try to do this with as little tension as possible. Make sure that your knees are unlocked.

In a circle, first person says a word. Second person makes a sound evoked by the word. Third person says a new word. Next person makes an associated sound. And so on.

Recall an occasion when you were lost. How was it solved.

Talk about the occasion.

RESPONSE TASK: create as many spaces on a large sheet of paper as there are group members. When a memory has been told, reflect on 'how' you could remember this story. What is the key? Then make a small drawing to support your memory in one of the spaces. This is called a 'mnemonic' drawing.

Share some of the symbols you have used.

Tell the story 'Riverturtle Is Not Singing' up to: 'So what if you throw me into the sun? Mr Coyote got very angry with little Riverturtle.'

Discuss in pairs how the story progresses. Bear in mind that ultimately Riverturtle will be alive and well in the river which is home. Which adventures were lived through before this happened?

Create a mini-drama of your story-continuation.

Present your work.

Before discussing the presentations, write two statements: one reflecting Riverturtle's learning in your story version, the other reflecting your Coyote's learning.

Share these statements with the group and discuss the presentations.

Tell the story's original ending.

Reflect on the entire session.

Crow and Frog
ESCAPE FROM DANGER

Play 'Everyone who . . . ' In this game the room is divided into three sections. One represents 'yes', the opposite end 'no', the middle signifies 'sometimes or maybe'. One of the group members enters the middle and calls out: 'Everyone who likes . . . or dislikes . . . or has ever . . . or has never . . . '. Group members quickly choose positions in the appropriate sections. Then the next person asks a question, and so on. Examples might include: everyone who loves fairgrounds; everyone who has ever been stood up on a date; or everyone who has ever had a difficult neighbour.

Reflect a little on the exercise.

Group stands in a circle. One member begins a movement. The others imitate until someone brings about a change. People need to look at each other in order to notice who is changing the pattern. Exercise ends when group is ready to end it.

Tell the story of 'Crow and Frog'.

Imagine that both Crow and Frog keep a detailed daily diary. Write either Frog's or Crow's diary notes of that day's events.

RESPONSE TASK: redistribute the diary notes. Carefully read the text which you have just been given. Write the underlying text: what has not been said by this crow or frog. Which feelings were not admitted to? Which events were omitted altogether, given that you know the account of what happened? Return text and sub-text to the original author.

Read both texts.

Re-write the diary entry with these new notes in mind.

Read the final diary note in groups of three or four. Discuss what you changed/ added. Pay special attention to common elements and differences.

Return to the circle.

Discuss your experiences, referring to those aspects of the diary notes which are particularly relevant to you at this point in time.

Reflect upon the entire session.

The evil bet
WHEN WE LIE

Explore a range of rhythms through clapping. Clap in unison, in three or four small groups (different, complementary rhythms) and also clap whilst each group member holds their own beat. Make conscious use of silence in the clapping process.

Use finger paints to create the image evoked by the word 'lie'.

RESPONSE TASK: each person creates as many small pieces of paper as there are group members. Then place the finger paintings in such a way that members can walk around to have a look at them. Take your own small pieces of paper and a pen with you. Look at each painting. Focus on the feeling it evokes within you. Write this feeling on a piece of paper. Leave the paper with the painting. Do this also for your own work.

Return to your own painting. Read the feeling words which have been left near the painting. Select the ones which are important to you. Use these words to create a brief poem, e.g.

Smothered by stinking lies I carried on.

No way out. Merciless horrors surrounded me.

Pityful. Pityful. Pity me.

Place a drum in the middle of the circle. Before and after reciting their poem each group member will use the drum to evoke the spirit/rhythm of the poem and to enhance its ending. The drum is returned to the centre. The next group member takes the drum, and so on.

Tell the story of 'The Evil Bet'.

Remind yourself of lies which you have told and of the ways these have both protected and damaged you and others.

Discuss the impact of lies.

Reflect on the entire session.

The fishpond of Paaiea

WAYS OF COPING WITH REFUSAL

Establish hand contact. Focus on your breathing and focus simultaneously on the hands you are holding. Imagine that with your *left* hand you are reaching out towards your neighbour. Try to convey this in the way you explore their hand. Meanwhile your right hand will be greeted in a similar way by the person on your right. Make sure that you say goodbye carefully.

Create a chain drama. This goes as follows: There is an enactment area with one or two chairs. X and Y enter the area. Y has a reasonable request to make of X. X refuses and will not budge, even though Y argues a good case. With a final refusal X leaves the stage. Then Z enters. He/she has a reasonable request to make of Y, who refuses. Y leaves and A enters, etc. Until at last X enters to make the final request. When this too is refused, the chain drama ends.

Discuss what it felt like to have a reasonable request refused/to refuse.

Tell the story of 'The Fishpond of Paaiea'.

Suppose that you were asked to write the title for a song/poem/article which describes Kapulau's state of mind the day after the volcano has erupted. Such a caption might simply read: 'Kapulau's lament'.

Share the titles.

Create several small groups on the basis of the similarities between the titles.

Write a brief text to amplify Kapulau's state of mind. This text needs to be written for solo voice and a chorus. Rehearse your chanted song-text.

Present your work to the group.

RESPONSE TASK: paint a gift of comfort and encouragement for Kapulau. **Share** these gifts with each other.

Reflect upon the entire session.

When Emu and Wild Turkey inflicted grief
AN EXPLORATION OF BITTER ENVY

Reflect on compliments which you have received. Select one or two which you are willing to share with the group.

Take a small lump of clay. Let your mind focus on feelings of envy and jealousy. Remind yourself of those occasions when you have felt envious or jealous. Use the clay to mould and unmould masks of envy. End your work by shaping the clay into a ball.

Write a list of the kinds of jealousies which you have experienced.

Share some of these with the group.

Tell the story of 'When Emu and Wild Turkey Inflicted Grief'.

Take a little more clay if you want to. Then create a shape which reflects your response to the story.

Find a partner: show your partner your clay shape. Partner will adopt a posture reflective of the clay shape. Then you will interact around the theme 'Make it a little better'. At times the betterment is first given form in the clay and then reflected in your body shape. At times the other way round. Work until a tolerable level of tension/feeling is achieved. Then change over.

Return to the circle.

Discuss your experiences.

Look at your earlier list of jealousies/envy.

Share some of these jealousies in a group of three or four. See if you can find the longing which lies at the root of the jealousy. What is it?

Discuss these longings/desires.

Reflect upon the entire session.

The animals argue about the length of day and night
THE WAY OF THINGS

Decide whether you will move like a grizzly bear, a rattlesnake or a big toad. Start moving through the room. After some time, seek out the other group members who are part of your animal family. Join a small group. Explore some of the sounds through which your animal group might interact. Allow yourself to be imaginative. Interact through sound and movement for a period of time until you feel familiar with your animal's sound language.

Then please, close your eyes and slowly move away from your group. Keep using your animal group's language. Other sounds will now surround you. Then, still with your eyes closed, imagine that you want to find the members of your own animal group. Search for them. Use your calls to establish contact and move towards each other. When your group is complete, open your eyes and sit down awhile to discuss the experience.

Tell the story 'The Animals Argue about the Length of Day and Night'.

With a partner draw a series of recurring patterns. Design the patterns together. Look at your work and stand up.

Translate your patterns into movements. Dance a shared dance.

Take a sheet of paper. Write at the top of the page:

> *That's how it is.*

And at the bottom of the page:

> *It is inevitable.*

Write the text which belongs in between those two sentences.

Read your texts.

RESPONSE TASK: after having listened to a text, finger-paint an image of the feeling evoked in you.

Share your painted responses.

Reflect upon the entire session.

A few questions to explore

○ When does speech become song?

○ Why is it difficult to measure the speed at which different animals move? How fast or slow is the tortoise?

○ How are shadows made?

○ Why should desert animals move about quickly during daytime?

○ How do turtles defend themselves against danger?

○ What is special about the coyote?

○ How does a crow catch its food?

○ What types of 'well' do you know? How is a well struck?

○ In which different ways do communities organise the use of wells?

○ What is meant by a food chain? Describe the food chain from frog to crow.

○ What is a city?

○ How is life in a city organised?

○ What are volcanoes and where do they occur?

○ How can we explain that some volcanoes, like those in Hawaii, lie far from plate edges?

○ How can volcanic eruptions be predicted?

○ Where are some of the world's richest fishing grounds?

○ To which danger are these fishing grounds exposed?

○ What is meant by a 'fishing season'?

○ What are traditional and modern ways of preserving fish?

○ Why can the emu not fly? Which other birds cannot fly either?

○ How do animals and people control the number of children they will have? Which methods do they use?

○ What determines the length of day and night?

○ Which different methods of time measurement do you know?

FOUR

THE LIGHT IS GREY

Yet wee, as if some foes were here,
Leave the despised Fields to clownes,
And come to save our selves as twere
In walled Townes.
Sir Richard Fanshawe

The group understood that change at a multiplicity of levels was unavoidable. Internal change as well as external change had to be simultaneously pursued. In fact they were intrinsically linked. This insight informed a new commitment, though the task felt overwhelming in its complexity. A lot of water flowed under the bridge. There was a profound longing for actual manifestations, if not demonstrations, of the renewed intention to make change happen. Not just through membership of the group, or through having stuck with it during the various ups and downs, but through tangible evidence in changed ways of relating and acting.

At this stage therefore we begin to acknowledge that in spite of our felt sense of inadequacy, we do contribute to group cohesiveness. Our commitment is noted. Somehow the group grows to be more comfortable with the shifting patterns of leadership. So everyone's energy now has a channel as well as a focus, which is mutually agreed and supported, at least more often than not. Anticipatory anxiety diminishes when we surrender rigid patterns of self-perception. Some of the peripheral symptoms of confused group functioning have been resolved. Increased understanding of the various upheavals, which run through the group at predictable intervals, is being applied. Thereby strength is gained.

The extent to which the actual group experience is the testing ground for the kind of changes we desire to bring about elsewhere, is truly surprising. How could we have anticipated that the process within the group reflects so intimately the process set in motion in other places and with other people. This reflective connection is at once disturbing and encouraging. Disturbing because it makes our own learning all the more crucial, and consequent failure even more dramatic. Reassuring because it provides us with the confidence of achievement. If it can be achieved here, then – in all likelihood – it can be achieved in other circumstances. Provided we are able to understand the conditions under which change is brought about.

Once in a while group members begin to question whether skills can really be transferred in this way. To discuss various ways by which what is learned through the participation in the group process can be applied in those numerous other situations in which we are involved. The earlier willingness to explore plausible as well as possible explanations for events is beginning to yield rewards. Because some of the dynamics of the situation we have experienced were conscientiously brought into focus, we discover the dynamics of group process. This understanding contributes to an easing out of our tension.

We keep having to learn that rigid a priori plans do not work. That preparation and planning for change demand foresight, the formulation of alternative action strategies and flexibility in the process of implementation. This strategic and intentional flexibility is hard to acquire. We still struggle with wanting to get it right through prediction. The realisation that although difficulties can be anticipated, they cannot be controlled, still meets with substantial resistance. How do you rehearse such flexible anticipation? Some people suggest that maybe we are in the wrong group and that all of us should learn an ancient martial art. The very suggestion is helpful.

The processes of problem clarification seem to be endless and lead, just by themselves, to ever new experiences of the problems. Like the tortoise and the hare in Aesop's fable, they also never quite catch up with each other. As in the fable, this makes no actual sense. But it feels right.

The growing trust in the process of change enables us to note our anxiety. We have experienced concerns about our wobbly motivation. However, we have not yet addressed our realisation that we do not possess some of the skills which are required of us. Or that we genuinely believe that we do not have the internal resources to acquire those skills. In other words: that there are actual limits to our capabilities. This is tough, for it reminds us of passing exams and 'effort is all that matters'. Whilst we had simply wanted to have an 'A' with or without effort.

Our capacity to act can be trained to the utmost, but we also know that there are limits. There are some things which we cannot do which others can do. Actual limits. The seemingly relentless optimism about limitless abilities and resources, which now pervades the group, is getting us down. Our protected try-outs at bringing about change are encouraging. We admit as much. But our new reality orientation demands that others too acknowledge that there are no magical ways out. We will keep on trying. We shall keep on dreaming and hope not to play truant when something bad has happened. To own up to the reality of our experiences.

However, somehow and at some time our actual limits must be recognised. Otherwise we will feel not only out on a limb, but also out in the cold. To be out in the cold once again feels unbearable. Therefore it is truly helpful if at this stage the skills which are demanded of us, and the skills which we have, are clarified. We can then bring to the fore those skills which we do not possess and those which we may have difficulty acquiring. It is rather painful to do this yet simultaneously an infinite relief. The effort to change is a real struggle. Together we are learning how to go about it. Ways of clarifying, tolerating and setting limits appear to be a crucial part of the process. The cost of not undertaking this task is too great.

1 The twelve months

A LONG TIME AGO on a remote farm there lived a widow who had two daughters. One was her own child, the other a stepdaughter. The widow loved her own daughter very much; her stepdaughter she loathed with fierce anger. The stepdaughter had to do all the work on the farm, whilst the older girl spent her entire day in idle vanity. The mother and daughter hated the young girl all the more because she never complained. However harshly they treated her, she remained kind. When they could not stand her pleasant compliance any longer, the furious twosome decided to do away with the stranger in their home.

One day in January, when frost held the ground in tight embrace and snow covered even the tallest bushes, the older girl said to her stepsister: 'Go into the forest and pick me some violets. Don't you dare come back without them. I won't let you back into the house until you have some beautiful violets.'

The young girl protested. How could she possibly find violets in January? But before she had even finished speaking she was thrown out of the house. She walked and she wandered, knowing full well that if she lay down, she would die. Heavy snow clouds darkened the sky, when suddenly in the far distance, on top of a small hill, she saw a fire. Her little body frozen with cold, she hurried towards it. When she reached the top of the hill she saw twelve people sitting on rocks around a huge fire. They were the twelve months.

The sight of the twelve people frightened the girl. She did not know who they were or why they kept their silent vigil by the side of the fire. They did not seem to notice her. It took all her courage to say: 'May I warm myself by your fire please? I am very cold.'

The oldest of the people turned towards her. Kind eyes rested upon the frozen girl. January asked: 'Will you tell us what has brought you into the forest at this time of the year?'

Worry furrowed her little face. She said: 'I have been sent to pick violets.'

January frowned: 'Violets don't blossom in winter, my child.'

The girl helplessly replied: 'I know . . . I know. But the farm doors have been barred behind me. My stepsister threw me out into the forest to pick some. I cannot go back until I find the violets. Can't you tell me where they grow? Please?'

January looked around the circle and said: 'March, will you take my seat?' The rod which January had been holding was passed to March who hurried towards the tallest rock where until then January had been seated. The fire was stirred and flames leapt up. The snow was melted. Catkins appeared. Then soft green leaves. A new light shone in the grass. Beneath the bushes violets sprang forth. A huge carpet of blue violets covered the ground.

March looked at the young girl who had been watching the changes in amazement. 'Do not forget to pick your violets my child.' March had a kindly voice. She gathered the violets, as many as she could hold in her hands and having thanked the twelve people, she ran home.

The angry twosome was not pleased to see her come back clasping a bunch of beautiful violets. The next day they sent her out of the house again, barking: 'Don't you get back till you bring us some strawberries.' She wept and protested, but it was to no avail. Once more she roamed the frozen forest. She searched for the fire, but could not find it. When she had given up all hope of ever finding the friendly circle, she noticed the light on top of the hill. Dragging her

feet through the snow, she stumbled towards it. She saw the vener-
able January sitting upon the tallest rock whilst the low flames glowed
in the winter light.

Again the girl asked: 'Please, may I warm myself by your fire? I am
so cold.' January looked at her. Seeing the kind concern, she said:
'They took the violets and threw me out again. They want
strawberries.'

'Strawberries in winter, my child?'

'I won't be let into the house again unless I bring them
strawberries.'

January left the tallest rock and walked halfway round the circle.
The beautiful rod was handed to June: 'Will you take my place?' asked
January.

June hastened towards the tallest rock and passionately stirred the
low flames. They jumped towards the sky. Snow melted, the trees
were dressed in leaves and blossom, birds sang and built their nests.
Summer came. Beneath the beech tree myriad white flowers
blossomed. Red fruits appeared. At last the ground was covered with
wild strawberries. June looked at the girl who dared not touch the
sparkling fruit: 'Do not forget to pick the fruit, my child.' She heard
the voice and filled her small apron with juicy strawberries. Her dark
eyes shone as she thanked the twelve people. Then she hurried
home.

Her stepsister and mother were astonished. How come she had
again defeated their purpose? They greedily ate the strawberries and
straightaway threw her out again. 'Don't you dare dirty this house
with your feet unless you bring us some wonderful apples. Don't get
anywhere near here without apples.'

Tired to the bone she returned to the forest. As no fresh snow had
fallen she could still see the shadow of her footsteps. It was only a
little while since she had rushed home, her apron filled with the
strawberries mysteriously granted by the people on top of the hill.
She followed her footsteps' trail. When she arrived at the circle of
fire, the people greeted her with concern and before she could speak,
they asked what her angry mother and stepsister demanded this time.
With a timid voice she told them about the apples.

January rose. Without another word the rod was handed to

September. Once more she witnessed the stirring of the fire and the melting of the snow. Autumn crocuses dressed the hills in gentle purple and rosehips swayed on the bushes. Then she saw the apple tree. Apples growing on every blessed branch. Two were within her reach. She picked these two and glanced at the twelve people in grateful astonishment. 'Hurry home now,' said September, 'and don't look back.'

She ran home, for darkness was falling fast. When she returned with two shining apples, her stepmother and sister could not believe their eyes. They demanded to know where she had picked them. The girl spoke the truth when she said: 'On the hill in the forest. There are lots more apples in the forest.'

'How come you only brought us two apples, then?'

'Because I was not tall enough. I could only reach these two.'

They ate her apples and as they could not make her grow tall overnight, they decided to go into the forest themselves to gather the other apples. They set out and after they had wandered through the forest a long, long time they too saw the circle of twelve people. They walked towards the fire and without further ado began to warm themselves. When January enquired whence they came and what they wanted, the girl answered: 'Why should I tell you? Move back a little. I want to warm myself.' January drew back. The flames became smaller and smaller. Fierce snowstorms rushed through the skies.

They never found their way back to the cottage. The kind-hearted girl waited for them for a long, long time. They did not return. Time passed. The girl grew into a delightful young woman and lived happily more often than not.

2   Rohini's wisdom

A LONG TIME AGO in a faraway city there lived a rich man. It was the time of winter. One day this man made it known that he would pay one thousand golden coins to the first person who was able to stand knee-deep in the river during the twelve hours of darkness. No warm clothes would be allowed, no refreshments or warm drinks either. The test was a simple one. A person had to wade into the river at the hour of dusk dressed only in a thin summer outfit and remain standing for twelve hours. As it was the middle of winter the water was very cold.

Outside the city there lived a poor man and his daughter. Her name was Rohini. They too heard of the rich merchant's challenge. The poor man hastened to the city. He wanted to be the first to accept the offer. He asked to see the rich merchant and announced that he wanted to meet the challenge that very night. The merchant saw the poor, shivering man. He laughed and tried to convince him that he would not even be able to stand in the river for five minutes, let alone for twelve hours, but the poor man did not change his mind. He wanted to make the attempt. It was his right.

Thus it happened that on the agreed hour the poor man descended towards the water. It was flowing fast and bitterly cold. The man waded away from the bank until the water reached his knees. He stood and waited till morning came. When twelve hours had passed he climbed out of the river and made his slow, painful way to the merchant's house.

The rich merchant knew that the man had passed the test, but he no longer wished to part with his money. He therefore asked how the man had been able to withstand the cold of night. 'Sir, I noticed that nearby a lamp was burning. I did not take my eyes away from it. Thus I received the strength to endure the cold.'

'Well!' said the merchant. 'You are a dishonest person. The light of the lamp kept you warm. You failed the challenge. I cannot possibly give you the reward.'

With these words he dismissed the poor man, who bowed his head in horror. He could find no words for his feelings. It had been a long night. He made his way back to the humble dwelling outside the city walls where Rohini awaited him. Of course she saw that something had happened to her father and when she heard the full story she was determined to confront the rich merchant. She went to his house carrying a jug full of fresh water and asked to see him.

The merchant was surprised to see the young girl and even more surprised that she was carrying a simple jug as if it were most precious to her. He invited her to speak. The girl said: 'Sir, if I tell you that

from this time onwards you may merely quench your thirst by looking
at the water in this jug, then what will be your response?'

'I shall tell you that I would rather drink it. It might make a
difference, mightn't it . . . ?' the merchant indulgently replied.

'Then, how could you expect my poor father, who did meet your
challenge and who was able to stand knee-deep in the river for twelve
hours dressed in nothing but summer clothes, to be kept warm merely
by looking at a lamp which stood on the river bank? How could you
believe such a thing.'

When the merchant's eyes met those of the young girl he felt his
insincerity. He called for her father and paid the man the promised
reward. Rohini and her father lived together for some years more.

3   The chief of the smiths who could not make human beings

I N THE OLD DAYS there lived a king. The king sent for Walukaga,
the chief of the smiths. He pointed to a big heap of iron and said:
'Use the iron to make a real person for me. Someone who can run as
well as walk, who can talk or keep silent, who has blood and bones,
but above all brains.'

The chief of the smiths, Walukaga, did not know what to do, but
he accepted the gifts of iron and made his way home. He asked many
people, the wise ones too. However, none of these were able to help.
They did not know how he could succeed in his task, how to make a
real person out of iron. He went from friend to friend; again and again
he told the story of the human being the king had asked him to make.
He showed them the iron, and pleaded for a solution. His friends
could not help him, even though they knew that Walukaga would be
severely punished for not obeying the king's instructions.

One day Walukaga visited a nearby village. Here his friends had
wept for him but given him no answer. On the way home he met a
man. He hardly recognised his former friend, which was not surprising for it had been a long time since the friend had been cast from the

village where he lived because he had become sick and confused. The people had ruthlessly forced him out of the village-compound. He had to live in the wild land. Walukaga approached his old friend and offered his greetings. The sick man asked about the purpose of Walukaga's journey. 'So what if he is often confused?' Walukaga said to himself. 'He is my friend. I want him to know what is happening.'

Then he told his story. How he had been called to see the king and instructed to create a human being who could talk and walk out of a heap of iron. He recounted too his hopeless journey from village to village in search of help with his predicament. No one had been able to offer him any guidance. They merely offered him consolation. What good did that do?

The sick man listened attentively. Then he said: 'The king has told you to make a human being. Return to his court and let it be known that in order to forge a fine human being, you need his assistance. Suggest that he issues a degree, which forces every person in the kingdom to burn their hair. Tell him you need a thousand loads of charcoal from burnt human hair. Tell him too that you shall need one hundred large pots of special water. This water has to be collected from human tears. It must be used to soften your fire and prevent it from burning too fiercely.'

Walukaga thanked his friend. Immediately he made his way to the palace where he requested to be given an audience with the king. He said: 'Sir, I have given your instruction much thought. I have learned how the task may be undertaken. I shall be able to use the iron which you provided to make a human being as you have suggested. However, I do need a thousand loads of charcoal of burnt human hair, which I shall use to transform the iron into a person. You must also instruct the people to weep many tears. I shall need a hundred pots full of this special water if I am to succeed with the task you require of me.' The king agreed to Walukaga's request. The people were told to shave their heads and to collect their tears. The burning of their hair only produced one load of charcoal and though they wept profusely at the king's command, they could only fill two pots of tears.

The king saw that his people were doing their best, shaving their heads as soon as hair appeared and crying day and night. After some time he called Walukaga, the chief of smiths, and said: 'I withdraw my order. I have failed to collect what you need. I cannot provide you with the charcoal of human hair nor with the water of tears.' Walukaga fell to his knees and thanked the king. When he rose again he said: 'Sir, I requested the charcoal and the tears because I knew it could not be done. Our tasks were impossible.'

The other people gathered in that place and laughed. They said: 'Walukaga has spoken the truth.'

4 The buried moon

I N THE OLD DAYS there were bogs where the water was blackish green and the land soft and squirty. It was dangerous to walk through the bogs. One wrongly measured step and instead of landing on a spongy mool, you fell. Then you were as likely as not to drown in great pools of murky water. The bogs were a treacherous place.

Well, in that time the moon shone up above. You say that this was not unusual. However, you may not remember what happened during the moon's three dark nights. Let me tell you. Whenever the moon hid her face in the sombre cloak, the bog changed. Each day and every night the bog was a tricky place to walk about in, but during those three particular nights it was the foulest terrain you could ever be forced to go through. Evil horrors emerged from the sucking waters. Then all things vile which thrive on darkness crept through the gloom-riveted air.

Soon Moon heard what happened in the bog whenever she disappeared. She was worried, for she liked people. It did not take her long to decide that she had to travel to earth to discover for herself how bad things were. She dressed in her black-hooded cloak. Not even one shining hair could be seen. She seemed a small woman when she stood by the side of the bog. It was dark. The stars did their best to lighten her journey, but there wasn't much they could do. Moon heard the lapping, swishing sound of the water. She saw the scraggly tussocks and felt the darkness closing around her fragile body. It soaked into her. She trembled and was afraid.

Wishing that she had never descended to earth, she wanted to go back, but bogs will not let you go back. Once you enter, they will not let you go. You cannot even turn around on one of those small mools. Moon made another step and another. The water swished about her. She could feel the marsh sucking at her feet. The cloak's wet hem stuck to her ankle. Then her foot slipped. The gruesome water beckoned. She grabbed wildly about her. Groping about to steady herself, she clung to a snag and it ferociously clung to her, cutting into her slender wrists. Her hood slid over her terrified face. There was nothing she could do.

Then Moon heard a pitiful sound, the woeful call of a terrified man who knows that he is lost and perilously close to death. The sobs came nearer. Still the man stumbled from tuft to tuft, but Moon knew with two more steps he too would fall into the great gaping hole which sucked at her feet. She struggled even harder to get free, to lift her head from beneath the heavy hood. She twisted and turned. The snag's maddening grip grew tighter and tighter around her wrist. At last her hood fell back. A great light shone across the marsh. The

man thanked the Lord for the miracle that saved his life and hastened home. He did not look twice at the light which had so suddenly appeared to guide his way, nor did he give it a second thought.

Moon gasped with relief that the man was saved. Then she cried with all her heart. She so wanted to go with the man. Wanted to be saved from the dreaded bog. She pulled and called till she was exhausted. When the hood covered her face again, the light went out. The evil creatures of the bog returned. They howled and screeched. They beat her and snarled at her goodness. Mocked her for having rescued their night's prey. The dark witches and all things nasty joined together to smother the kindly moon. If only she had never left her place in the sky.

As she grew tired of the shouting and weary with fear, she felt how a thousand cruel hands dragged her down, further and even further down. The evil creatures laid her deep at the foot of the bog and placed the biggest stone they could find on top of her. They grinned with pleasure: the bog would be theirs alone night after lonesome night. Meanwhile the moon lay buried. Would anyone know where to look for her?

Well, time passed and the people waited for the birth of the new moon. They were glad when the dark time was over. Now the blessed light would return to banish the evil things from the bog. Time passed, but the moon did not return. The evil things were nastier than ever. Why did the new moon not come? The people grew frightened. They searched amongst themselves for an answer; some asked the old people and a few strayed towards the woman in the mill to ask if by chance she had dreamt where the moon had wandered to. She did not know either. This was mighty odd.

The people got to know a fear such as until then they had only felt in the bog. The dark nights were everywhere. They talked and talked with each other, but they were no nearer to finding the moon. Then one evening the wandering man remembered the time he lost his way in the bog. How he had cried because death was pulling at his feet. He saw again the light which had shone before him. He knew at once: he had seen the moon. She had been lost whilst rescuing him.

When he told the people, they took him to the woman in the mill who listened and said: 'Aye, aye, the moon's in a bad way. Do as I say and all will be well. But remember, do *exactly* as I say. Gather a stone and a hazel twig and go to the bog when the light of day is grey and turning towards night. Put the stone in your mouth and take the twig in your hands. Don't speak a word till you get home again. Do not be frightened. In the middle of the bog you will see a cross, a candle and a coffin. I reckon you'll find her near there, but you must look for her.'

When the light was grey and night had not yet fallen, the people went into the bog. In spite of what the old woman had said, they were very frightened, for the evil things wailed and pulled. They did not speak, though, and they kept the stone between their chattering teeth. Suddenly they saw the cross, the coffin and the candle, or something like it, just as the old woman had foretold, but the moon was nowhere to be seen. Their eyes knew the bog. They recognised the snag all right – and the stone – and even the small flickering light.

The bravest amongst them went closer and grabbed the big stone. Some say that for a tiny minute they gazed at a beautiful cold face. She must have been so weary lying there beneath that heavy stone. Frightened too. The people had to close their eyes – they could not do otherwise – and when next they looked they saw the Full Moon in the Sky. That's how many nights had passed. She was smiling again, smiling very warmly and by her light the people returned. They no longer stood in the darkness just waiting. The moon had not forgotten them and they remembered her. The evil things were never the same again.

5 Nana Miriam

I N THOSE DAYS Fara Maka lived by the side of the River Niger. Even though he was tall and strong the people called him ugly. He was a member of the Songai tribe. This man had one daughter by the name of Nana Miriam. She was also tall and strong, but contrary to her father she possessed striking beauty.

When Nana Miriam was a child, she and her father had been inseparable. Fara Maka taught her many things, such as the way fish live in the river. Because she was a curious girl Nana Miriam wanted to learn the names of even the smallest and rarest fish, bestowing on each one the blessing of recognition. At other times they travelled deep into the forest. Here she became one-knowing with the ways of the animals and discovered how to call forth the healing power of shrubs and herbs.

Anyone who saw the girl was touched by her radiant vigour, yet unsuspecting of her magic powers. Her gaze was too innocent and her manner too ordinary. But Fara Maka, the ugly one, he saw it in his daughter's eyes and decided to share his own magic spells with her. Soon Nana Miriam became the most powerful young woman in the land of Songai.

At that time there lived by the side of the great River Niger a monster, who terrorised the villagers. It looked like a hippopotamus, but sometimes the monster would change into other forms. Each one terrible to behold. This monster was insatiable. It trampled the fields and devoured the meagre crops. Famine came to the Songai tribe. Of course the hunters tried to kill the monster. Every one of them had tried. However, their brave efforts were to no avail. Before their spears and arrows even touched the beast, it had changed shape. It was invulnerable.

Then Fara Maka decided that he too would attempt to defeat the monster's unrestrained might. He prepared to attack, but when he saw the fire which sprang from the beast's throat, the lonesome Fara Maka recoiled in fear. He drew breath and rushed forward again, calling upon his best magic protection as well as his spear not to fail him. His spear did not even touch the beast. The hippopotamus gazed scornfully at the foolish man. With a heavy heart Fara Maka made his way back to the village. The monster continued to ravage the fields and famine kept the people in strangulating embrace.

Fara Maka thought a long, long time. Then he approached one of the great dog-hunters of the Tomma tribe. Would he be prepared to kill the ever-changing hippopotamus aided by his many dogs? The hunter agreed. After having been given much food, he set out on the path to victory. The monster hippopotamus mauled the dogs, one after the other and the greatest hunter of the Tomma tribe fled.

Then Fara Maka abandoned his courage. When Nana Miriam saw her father's limp surrender, she knew that his attempts to kill the insatiable beast had failed. Maybe the whole village had to move further down river. Maybe the people's gardens had to be destroyed, but the girl refused to accept these thoughts. Something had to be done. She had to act. She spoke and said: 'Great men have tried to kill the hippopotamus. They failed. Father, I shall kill the monster.'

She went and found the monster's dwelling place. Day after day she quietly observed its every way. Then the hour came when she let herself be seen. The hippopotamus looked at her as if to say, 'I knew you were here. You want to kill me. Great men have tried; you are a girl. Don't even bother. How could you succeed?'

Nana Miriam returned his gaze undaunted. The fight began in earnest when the hippopotamus spat fire, but Nana Miriam changed the fire to water. He cast an impenetrable iron shield around himself. Nana Miriam shattered it. Then the hippopotamus felt fear such as it had not known before. Nana Miriam had grown to expect the monster's decoys and when the hippopotamus turned itself into a gently flowing river, she gathered the river and reshaped the hippopotamus. Once more she faced the awesome beast.

Meanwhile Fara Maka had gone in search of his daughter. He spotted Nana Miriam and the hippopotamus standing in gruesome bond by the side of the river. The monster heard a rustle. He looked around and upon seeing the lonesome one, he charged him blindly. Nana Miriam rushed after the beast. She lunged forward, grasped one of the monster's legs and with all her strength flung it across the river, where its head crashed against the further bank. The monster died.

Soon everyone in the tribe knew of Nana Miriam's deeds. The minstrel folk, the Dialli, composed a song to celebrate the power of Nana Miriam, the young woman who used her strength.

6   *Fish in the forest*

W HEN DIGGING her meagre land a woman found a treasure. She took it home and showed it to her husband. 'Look,' she said, 'Heaven has sent us great good fortune. We must hide it somewhere. But where?' Her husband suggested that they bury it in their cottage. They dug a hole in the floor and concealed their good luck. A little later the husband went out to meet his friends. The woman wondered what he would tell them, especially as she knew that he was unable to keep a secret. His tongue was as loose as the wind on a stormy day. Before night had fallen everyone in the village would know how lucky she had been.

Whilst her husband was out of the house, she opened the hole in the floor again and took the treasure to her secret hiding place in the chicken run. When the man came back home later that evening, she said: 'Tomorrow I want you to come with me. We are going to the forest to gather fish. The other women tell me that there are a lot of fish in the forest. We only have to gather them. You come with me.' The man laughed: 'Fish in the forest?' With a hint of sharpness in her voice she said: 'The other women found them there. They told me so. You had better come with me.'

The next morning the woman got up very early. From the larder she took a few fish and a hare which they had stored for lean days, and put them in a basket. Then she hurried to the baker, where she bought sweet cakes. When the cakes had joined the hare and the fish in the basket, the woman made her way to the forest. She looked about. No one to be seen. Carefully she placed the fish amongst some bushes along the path she intended to walk later that morning with her husband. The cakes were hung from a tree. Onwards to the river where she slung the hare on to a fishing hook and line. She set the line and cast the hare into the water. Well contented, she made her way home.

After breakfast the woman reminded her husband of the planned trip to the forest. They had not ventured very deep into the woods when they found a perch, then a pike and a carp. They were lying on the ground. If her husband was surprised he did not show it. He just

picked the fish up and put them in the basket. Then the man saw the
pear tree. It was richly laden with the sweetest cakes. The man loved
sweet cakes and exclaimed: 'Look at these cakes. How strange, sweet
cakes on a pear tree.' The woman simply answered, 'It does happen. I
have known this tree to be laden with cakes before now. The women
tell me that sometimes the rain brings these cakes. They've seen it
too.' The couple decided to go home. Their journey had been richly
rewarded.

On their way home they passed a small river. 'Wait a minute,' said
the husband, 'Look, there is a fishing line. There is no one near it.
I'm sure something is caught on that line. I cannot believe my eyes.
Look wife, look! There's a hare on that line. A hare . . . !'

'That's not unusual,' said she. 'The other women have often told
me how their husbands catch hare in the river. Well . . . you never go
fishing. Do you?!' Her husband did not speak another word. He did
not like the forest. It frightened him.

When they came home, they made ready to eat. It was a rich meal.
Soon the news that the woman had found a treasure whilst digging
the land had reached every ear in the village. The landowner too
heard the rumour. Wanting to know exactly what had happened he
summoned the woman and her husband to the castle. First he had a
word with the man. Then he called the woman. 'Be careful to speak
the truth,' the rich man said, 'for your husband has told me
everything. You have found a treasure.'

'No, my lord,' the woman replied.

'Don't deceive me, dear lady. I have warned you. Your husband
says you buried it beneath the cottage floor.'

'Have mercy, my lord,' the woman retorted. 'My husband does not
know what he says. He has been a bit unusual for some time now.'

Her husband looked outraged. 'I do know what I'm saying. I'm
speaking the truth. You did find a treasure.'

'Well, if you are certain, tell the lord when I found that treasure.
When was it?'

The poor man confidently replied: 'I remember. It was the day
before we found the fish in the forest. There were cakes on the pear
tree. It had rained sweet cakes. Remember? And then I fished the
hare out of the river. True?'

The woman looked at the lord of the castle as if to say, 'What did I tell you?' He sent them both home. Of course the cottage floor was dug up, but the labourers did not find anything. The rumours died away.

What the woman eventually did with her treasure is another story.

Working with the stories

The twelve months

A LESSON LEARNED?

Write one sentence evoked by the word 'season'.

Read these sentences.

Recall any songs/melodies/music related to seasons.

Share your memories.

Sing or hum some of these songs.

Talk about food/plants/activities which nowadays can be eaten/purchased/ undertaken irrespective of the time of year. Make a list of these. Reflect on the losses/gains of this situation.

Join one of four groups, either Spring, Summer, Autumn or Winter. Talk a little about the images/memories evoked by the season you have chosen. Then explore your theme through movement/improvisation. Prepare a brief presentation. Sequence your presentations. Let the work 'flow' from one group to the next by freezing your closing posture. The next group imitates the posture and continues the work from there. As soon as a posture has been imitated, the group concerned unfreezes their posture and witnesses the next season's presentation.

Reflect on your experience.

Tell the story 'The Twelve Months'.

Ponder the story for a while, especially those moments which are meaningful for you. Then select one sentence from the story which still resonates. Write this sentence on a piece of paper. Take about 5 minutes to record thoughts, memories or associations which are evoked by this sentence.

Sequence the sentences which have been chosen in accordance with their place within the story.

Read your writings in this sequence.

RESPONSE TASK: create as many small pieces of paper as there are group members. After having listened, reflect on what kind of lesson can be drawn from the experience. Write this down. When everyone has shared their writings, distribute the 'lessons to be learned'.

Read what you have received.

Select one or two 'lessons' which feel pertinent to your own life situation.

Share these with the group.

Reflect on the entire session.

Rohini's wisdom

DIGNIFIED OUTRAGE

Complete the following sentences:
'When I feel good I . . . '
'When I feel bad I . . . '
Do this as many times as feels right.

Sit in pairs facing your partner. Establish eye contact. Ponder what it is this person might like. Talk for two minutes about your ideas. Try not to give your partner feedback about the accuracy/inaccuracy of their perceptions. Before discussing the experience, change over.

Reflect on the imagined likes. Discuss which ones you recognise, and which ones you don't recognise. Talk also about how it felt to have someone imagine such things about you.

With a new partner, create a list of personal endurance records, e.g. the longest walk (when/where); the most uncomfortable night (when/where); the longest period of silence, etc.

Return to the circle and share your lists.

Tell the story 'Rohini's wisdom'.

Silently recall incidents when you or someone you love was unfairly treated. Irrespective of whether you said so at the time.

Write about one of these incidents. End your writing with the sentence 'It was not fair . . . '

Place a chair in front of the group. In turn group members use this chair to read their writings and to present their 'It was not fair . . . ' incident to the group.

RESPONSE TASK: listen to each statement and think about what would have been needed or should have been done in order to remedy the experienced unfairness. Record your thoughts. When everyone has read their writings, read through your list of amendments/compensations. See if you can discern a common theme or trend.

Share your ideas with the group.

Reflect upon the entire session.

The chief of the smiths who could not make human beings

THE ADVICE OF THE EXCLUDED

Paint the image of a basket or pot which you (could) really like.

Share your images.

Remind yourself of a time when you received helpful advice. What was it? Who gave it to you? Why did you need it? Talk a little about this experience.

Tell the story 'The chief of the smiths who could not make human beings'.

Imagine that the ill man has heard that his advice worked. After some deliberation he decides to write a letter to the villagers who have cast him out. Write this letter.

RESPONSE TASK: on a sheet of paper create as many spaces as there are group members. Listen to each letter as if you were a villager. Note your reaction to the letter. Record this response in one word. Then paint a small image of the feelings evoked by this word.

Share your responses.

Reflect on the entire session.

The buried moon

SLOW UNFOLDING

Talk about balloons; likes, dislikes and fears associated with balloons. Then distribute as many balloons as there are group members. These need to be blown up. Some group members may want assistance with this.

Play a little with your own balloon. Move about the space whilst trying to keep your balloon airborne. Send your balloon to other people. Receive and return their balloon. Work fast, then in slow motion.

After having put your balloon away, continue/repeat your earlier movement patterns. Interact with each other as if you were still trying to keep the balloons airborne. Freeze. Notice how you are standing and what you are feeling. Then return to the circle.

Tell the story 'The Buried Moon'.

Scatter yourselves about the room. Ensure there is ample space between yourself and other people. Work with your eyes closed. Very slowly fold your body into a really compact posture, as if you were a big stone. Hold this posture for a while. Then slowly make one unfolding movement. Freeze again. Then unfreeze. Make another small unfolding movement. Freeze. Note what you are feeling. Unfreeze. Make a minor movement. Freeze. Focus on feelings. Unfreeze. Make a small sound, or utter a word. Move a little more. Then very slowly and gradually, allow your movement to take you towards group members whose sound seems to be calling you. Still keep your eyes closed. When you feel that you are quite close, interact through sound whilst continuing your movement. If you want, open your eyes. Develop your movement/sound improvisation until you feel that a natural completion has been reached. Sit down and look around. Then lie down and rest a while.

Return to the circle.

Share your experiences. Focus on the images evoked by the story and by your movement/sound work.

Paint/write a small gift for Moon after her return to the sky.

Retrieve your balloon if possible.

Give this balloon and your gift to another group member.

Reflect upon the gift you have received and upon the entire session.

Nana Miriam

FROM FEAR TO COURAGE

Play 'Grandmother's Footsteps'. One group member volunteers to be 'grandmother' and stands facing a wall at one end of the room. The other members try to creep up behind her. Once in a while grandmother looks around. Whenever she sees someone move, that person must begin again. Having stood motionless when grandmother looks around, the others continue their journey towards her as soon as she again faces the wall. The first person to touch the wall undetected becomes grandmother. The game can then be played once more.

In pairs explore physical positions which reflect *fear* and *courage*.

Explore the movements which enable development from a physical position which reflects fear to one which reflects courage, and vice versa.

Talk about your experience.

Tell the story 'Nana Miriam'.

Ask group members to look at a pile of newspapers and to cut out headlines/words which resonate with the story.

Place these headlines/words on to a large sheet of paper as if you were creating a newspaper report. Add other words and phrases which immediately spring to mind. Then write a report of the incidents/experiences mentioned in the story.

Read your reports.

RESPONSE TASK: after having listened to a report, record one sentence which may serve as an encouragement to Nana Miriam if, at some future time, her strength is failing her.

Read your list of encouragements. Try saying to yourself 'I need to hear that . . .' as if you had written these sentences to offer yourself guidance and encouragement in the here and now.

Discuss your experiences/responses.

Reflect upon the entire session.

Fish in the forest
THE USES OF STRATEGY

Look at your hands and reflect on something you appreciate about them. Maybe their strength, softness or agility.

Share what you value about your hands with the group.

Sit in pairs facing each other. Establish eye contact. Imagine that the person opposite you has a hidden treasure, either literally or metaphorically speaking. He/she knows this. You simply have reason to believe it exists. Try to convey your awareness of this situation in your eyes. Do not speak about it. Let your eyes do the work.

Talk about your experience.

Join a group of three or four: discuss associations connected with the word 'strategy'. What is it? How can it be used? How do you use it? Then imagine that you have to teach a group of people about 'the uses of strategy'. Design a simple exercise which people can perform either individually, in pairs or in a group which will teach them something about the usefulness of strategy.

Teach the other group members your exercise(s).

Talk about your experience.

Tell the story 'Fish in the Forest'.

Discuss in pairs which lessons can be learned from the story. Remind yourself of the earlier 'Hidden treasure' exercise. Explore how you could apply strategy in relation to such a hidden treasure.

Return to the circle: share some of these ideas.

Reflect upon the entire session.

A few questions to explore

o What are seasons and how do you recognise them?

o How do people overcome seasonal restrictions? What are the various advantages and disadvantages of by-passing seasonal limitations?

o What is a river?

o What causes river levels and water temperatures to vary?

o What happens when people have been exposed to the cold for too long?

o What are physical endurance levels?

o How is iron mined?

o What are the laws related to people with mental illness in this country?

o How does a smith work a forge?

o What is hair made of? What are the functions of hair cover?

o What is a bog?

o Why are the bogs and wetlands in this country threatened?

o Why do bogs lack nitrogen?

o Describe the phases of the moon as seen from earth.

o How do mills work?

o What kinds of varied life can be found in and close to a river?

o Why does being able to name an animal or a plant matter?

o How does fear show itself in a human or an animal's body?

o Why does a hippopotamus stay in the water most of the day?

o How do people keep animals off the land used for vegetable growing?

o Which of these methods threaten the survival of animal species?

o What is meant by subsistence farming?

o How is bread/are cakes baked? What is the process?

o Which fishing methods do you know which can be used by one person?

o How do we discover what is 'natural'?

FIVE

IS THE CUP NOT FULL YET?

. . . But oh! Did I
Think deeply on it, what it is to die,
My pulses all would beat, I should not be
Drowned in this deluge of security.
PHILIP PAIN

Once individual limits have been clarified, the group is likely to go – again – through a period of apparent resistance. Having become familiar with some of the fears of individual members, we discern that these are often disguised as an underlying scepticism about the feasibility of fundamental change. This is the group's uncertainty. In other words, the achievability of the goals is repeatedly, but not necessarily explicitly, questioned. Such questioning may be realistic, given that earlier abundant optimism may have led the group to biting off more than it can chew. However, in all probability the goals are questioned, not because they are unrealistic, but because – with the goal in sight – group members realise that their fulfilment will lead to the making of actual sacrifices by both the group members and by the people with whom they share their lives.

Until then such sacrifices may have been spoken about, but they did not yet need to be made. Reaching the goal means making them. Even though the change process was initiated because the existence of a problem was recognised, we may not have acknowledged our investment in having it in the very first place. Many problems tend to gratify some of our needs and lead to patterns of behaviour with which we are familiar. Patterns which, if the goals are accomplished, would cease to exist. Anticipated loss, even of unwelcome experiences, hurts too. Consequently all groups which aim for change repeatedly manifest this tension between stated desires and actual behaviour. Though we may be genuinely in support of the intention to bring about change, sadly we are likely to underestimate how much we have invested in not changing.

The felt sense of required sacrifice is amplified by renewed concerns about the constraints under which we have to operate. We are not even sure whether or not people understand what our life is really like. What we are up against and why we must cling to existing gratifications. If only we could be offered some sympathy. A degree of compassion which suggests that other people have been there too and know that one is not just being bloody-minded, or giving up on ideals when results are about to be shown. We too invested a lot in change. We want and wanted a greener world. But we feel that the demands which are placed upon us have suddenly and unexpectedly increased, even though seemingly nothing has changed. It is just that the pull of those demands is felt more poignantly. Yes, we are compromising earlier ideals. Indeed, it can even be said that we do appear to betray the cause from time to time.

At this stage of the group process we are likely to ask ourselves why the group has to enter into open conflict about such matters. It seems to be drawing attention to itself, left, right and centre. Members are personalising issues related to fallability. The temptations of the consumer society are many, but we are not just bowing to those temptations. There are demands of family and friends, of a job which needs to be done, our own need for pleasure and ease which we have neglected. We have been trying to be good for too long, and need some easing. Doesn't anyone understand? We don't want to harden our heart, but we wish to go out and play now.

The pragmatists speak with understanding about fallibility. The idealists condemn it. We wonder how such an articulate group of people could ever have descended to these simplistic levels of thinking. Why does the group have to get caught up in worries about betrayal? Let alone speak about it to outsiders? It reminds us of adolescence all over again. There certainly seems to be quite a bit of actual pairing going on in the group. Courtship patterns are emerging. Though these couples are playing for real, however, they are very private about their involvement with each other. Is all our hope secretly invested in them?

A great deal of effort has been risked so far. The increased information, which the group now has at its fingertips, suggests that the motivation to bring about change, internally as well as externally, ought to be even stronger. But the circumstances of group life have imperceptibly altered. Somehow we understand the preference for soft options much better. The group is likely to feel utterly lost. Some people suggest that maybe the group should be dissolved. This hurts.

The wish for abandonment is counteracted by others who state that as far as change is concerned it is good enough to achieve a realistic level of stability. Compromise? It seems to be a dirty word for several participants who insist on obviously (obviously?) unfeasible change. Why has the feasibility of the proposed changes become such a hot issue at this stage of our process? The accusations, which are still flying backwards and forwards, focus on 'ignorance'. Some of which hits home. For the temptation to play ostrich looms large.

During this stage of the change process the group is likely to feel that there is no support anywhere, whilst it is torn apart by internal conflict and accusations of inadequacy. This is not a struggle for leadership, nor an attempt to create alternative schools; it is a sign that the group is drowning in fear and pain.

As if the internal trouble is not enough, just at this point of the process, the external situation neatly mirrors the internal felt reality. This tends to make matters worse. The rooms which are used for meetings are suddenly unavailable. The photocopier breaks down. The link person with the town hall leaves her job. Funding is cut. You name it, it happens. The little cultural island for change, which wonders whether it is actually a volcano about to erupt, finds that both internally and externally survival is made difficult.

Chances are that wherever we look, all we see is trouble. Nothing is going easy. The group can of course survive this stage provided it has access to understanding the dynamics of change, and provided a majority of people are willing to trust those experiences. If a sufficient number of group members are involved in bringing about change elsewhere, and if they share what is happening there, they will be much astounded and relieved to find that the apparent boycotting, confusion, and curtailment of fundamental resourcing, is happening just about everywhere at more or less the same time in more or less the same way. Then they will recognise that these are not conditions created by the flaws of the individual facilitator or by that particular bunch of people, but that these are manifestations or side effects of change processes.

With such reassurance in our hearts and at our fingertips our capacity to contain the apparent chaos increases. It is functional noise and rumble. The urge to protect newness then becomes nearly passionate. It *is* passionate. The pain has most certainly intensified, but once we make use of the support and advice we can offer each other, a great deal of strength is also gained. Of course there will be the occasional awareness of actual failure. We reproach ourselves when a task we performed could have been done a great deal better. But the reproaches become more reality-focused. Our judgments become less harsh and persecutory. We discover what reconciliation truly means.

During this very tough stage of the group process we deserve to be reminded that fundamental change is rarely easy, and that none of us are willing or even able to embrace such change wholeheartedly. When we realise this, we become a great deal more tolerant of frustration, learn to use containment as a way of waiting and as a method of coping. The fierce battles disappear. We primarily offer each other mutual support. Mistakes are acknowledged without being turned into tragedies. Ignorance becomes an opportunity for discovery. Thereby we manage to take yet another hurdle. Meanwhile our sense of humour has been granted some exercise.

1   When Hare heard of Death

WHEN HARE DISCOVERED DEATH he ran back to the place where he lived. He shouted and cried: 'My people must not die!' He imagined the sloping rocks. They fell away. He imagined the big mountains. They fell apart. He imagined the place below the earth. Everything that lived in the soil stopped scurrying about; all froze and died. He imagined the skies high above him. The birds which had been flying stopped flying and fell to earth, dead.

He crawled into the place where he lived. He reached for his blanket, and rolled himself into it. He lay there and wept. There will not be enough earth for all that dies, he thought. There is not enough earth for all that dies. He buried himself in his blanket. He made no sound.

2   How the elephant died

ONE DAY Hare noticed that some elephants were about to cross the river. They were going to visit the home of their inlaws. The biggest elephant carried a bag of honey on his back. Hare approached this one saying: 'Father, help me across. Let me get on your back. I am but a poor creature.' Elephant allowed Hare to climb on to his back and waded into the river, not knowing that as soon as they had left the river bank Hare opened the bag of honey. He ate the honey.

Whilst he was eating, some of it fell on to Elephant's back. Elephant felt those little drops and wondering what it was, he asked Hare, who replied: 'Father, those are the tears of a poor creature weeping.' When they arrived on the other shore Hare asked the elephants to find him some stones. He convinced them that he needed the stones to throw at the birds, who so often hunted him. Kindly the elephants searched the ground for stones. They lifted the stones to Hare who put them into the honey bag. When the bag was full Hare jumped off the Elephant's back. Hardly had his feet touched the ground when he dismissed his companions and helpmate.

The elephants trudged along until they came to the home of their inlaws. Here they opened the honey bag. As soon as they saw that the honey had been replaced by stones they went in pursuit of Hare, who was feeding not too far away. Fearing great danger Hare rushed into a hole, but the biggest elephant put his trunk into the hole, slung it around Hare's leg and pulled. Hare shouted laughingly: 'You slung your trunk around a root.' Elephant let go of Hare's leg. He twirled his trunk around the tree root which lay bare inside the hole. He pulled and pulled. Hare could be heard to weep: 'You have broken me. You have broken me.' The Elephant pulled even harder, until he became very tired. Because he was pulling so hard he did not notice how Hare had slipped out of the hole and sped away.

Whilst Hare was running along he spotted a group of baboons. He pleaded for help. Taking their time the baboons enquired what was

causing him to run with such great fear. Hare replied that he was
being chased by an enormous creature. The baboons comforted Hare
and offered to protect him. He no longer needed to be frightened.
Hare was given shelter in their home whilst they kept guard outside.
A little later Elephant came that way. He asked the baboons if they
had seen Hare. They pondered his question and demanded to know
what price he was willing to offer if they told him Hare's whereabouts.
Elephant said he would give them whatever they asked for.

They wanted a cup full of his blood. First he looked to see that the
cup was a small one, then Elephant consented. The baboons made a
hole in his neck and the Elephant's blood gushed forth. Time passed.
The baboons were still filling the cup and Elephant asked wearily: 'Is
the cup not full yet?' They showed it to him. It was only half full. The
baboons had made a hole in the bottom of the cup and whenever they
showed it to Elephant he saw that it was not full yet. The baboons
made fun of him. They said that he was lacking in courage. Could he
not even fill such a little cup with his own blood? They bled and bled
him. The cup was never filled. Elephant sank to the ground. There he
died. Hare was no longer frightened. He left his hiding place.

3   Nyambe leaves the earth

IN THE BEGINNING Nyambe lived on earth. He made everything:
trees, fish and reptiles, birds, animals and also people. Nyambe
lived with his wife Nasilele. One of Nyambe's creatures was a man
named Kamunu. He was different from the other creatures and very
clever, as clever as Nyambe himself. Whenever Nyambe made
something new, Kamunu did the same. If Nyambe carved a spoon,
Kamunu carved one too. Whatever Nyambe did, Kamunu faultlessly
imitated him: whether Nyambe smelted iron or built a hut, Kamunu
would do it in the same perfect way.

One day Nyambe saw how Kamunu had forged a spear and before
too long he used the spear to kill a male antelope. He ate the flesh,
liked it and killed another one and more. He would not stop. This
made Nyambe very angry. He reminded Kamunu that he was killing

his brothers and that he must not do this, but Kamunu would not listen and at last Nyambe drove him away. He sent him to a faraway land. Without Nyambe this land was not good for Kamunu. He was helpless. Then Nyambe gave Kamunu a garden. An eland wandered into Kamunu's garden at night. He took his spear, killed the eland and ate it. Nyambe was angry again. Kamunu explained how the eland had eaten the food in his garden and even though Nyambe did not like it that the eland had been killed, he did not punish Kamunu.

Then Kamunu's dog died, one of his pots broke and his child died too. He went to see Nyambe. He wanted to be given medicine to keep the things he wanted, to bring them back to life. Nyambe said: 'I can give you that medicine, but you must also use it to bring back to life all the things you kill.'

Kamunu did not like this thought and went away. He found another dog and this one also died. Before long he broke his new pot. So Kamunu went back to Nyambe to ask for medicine. However he still did not want to stop killing his brothers and sisters, the eland and the buffalo. Nyambe was still very angry. He tried to flee for he did not want to speak to Kamunu. But wherever Nyambe the creator fled, Kamunu had a way of finding him. This distressed Nyambe very much, for he really did not want to see Kamunu ever again.

Then Spider came to Nyambe. She built a thread towards the sky. Nyambe and Nasilele climbed up the thread. In the sky they found a place for themselves where they have stayed since then.

Kamunu knew that Nyambe had disappeared up there. He and the people built a high tower, for they wanted to ask Nyambe to show them something. They were stubborn. Nyambe was pleased that the tower could never be built high enough. It always collapsed. Since that time Kamunu cannot reach Nyambe. He can no longer be shown how to make newness. People still kill the eland and the buffalo and all the other animals.

Nyambe and Nasilele live beyond the clouds. They had to retreat.

4   The rice and the sugarcane

THEY SAY that Sugarcane sought the company of Rice. Sugarcane was looking for friendship and spoke as follows:

'I have come to see you for I with us to be friends as well as relatives. To share with you the harsh and troublesome times. We have sprung from one source. We are of kindred origin. Are we not produce of the earth? Though our likeness extends beyond these. Events befall us both and whatever is granted to us is bestowed equally upon us. Our lives are a verisimilitude, so is our death. Some people even give us names which sound alike. I suggest that we declare ourselves to be friends.'

It is said that Rice responded to Sugarcane's words in the following manner:

'Your words have a semblance of truth, especially when you hold forth regarding our origin. Indeed we are both produce of the soil. We are equal in life and can be compared to one another in death. All these truths I grant you. But there is nonetheless something which prevents me from accepting your proposal. Something about which we shall never agree. I can tell you now there is no place for friendship between us nor is there cause for blame. You needed to have thought this matter through more carefully. As you know, those who cavort with fishermen smell of fish. Those who befriend the wanderers are vagrants themselves and those who seek the company of labourers are themselves labourers. Dear friend, I have to decline your offer of friendship for ultimately you do not remain the same. For this reason alone we are prevented from entering into the bond of lasting companionship. As you know, we Rice do not endure transformations. Whatever befalls us we do not change. Let me be kind and explain this to you.

'You need to understand that we are moistened so that we may rot. When we are rotten, we are planted. Time passes, but still we are Rice. When we have greened, our roots are lifted and we are replanted where water flows freely. Yet, through all this we have not changed, we are still Rice. We grow and ripen. Then we are cut with a sharp knife. Though we are cut, we remain Rice. Once we have been gathered we are cast against a great stone. But we do not change, we remain Rice. Even when we are buried in the rice pit, we do not change. Let me remind you, we remain Rice. Kind hands lift us from the pit, we are laid out to dry in the sun. We may be pounded by the pestle, we may have our skins flayed from our core, yet through all this, we do not change, but remain Rice. Yes, let me assure you, when we are placed in the cooking pot and rest in boiling water, when a fierce fire burns beneath us, then too we know that we remain Rice. When people take us into their mouth to eat, they chew and swallow us. They swallow Rice. Thus many calamities may happen unto us, yet we do not change, we remain Rice. It is equally true that famine is banished from the land wherever we dwell. Many a place where we have not made our home is desolate.

'Let me now speak about you. As you know you are cut into small pieces and stuck in the earth. You have not changed. Of course you are still Sugarcane. Then you grow and sway in the wind, and once more you are cut. This does not yet change you, you are still called Sugarcane.

'People's teeth may chew you to fibre or you are crushed in the sugar mill: I know that you have not changed. You still deserve the name Sugarcane. Then you are thrown into a great pot, water is added and the pot is placed above a great fire. The water thickens. The fire is extinguished. Then you have changed, and people call you Sugar. Your journey does not end there, you are reheated and become vapour. You travel through a pipe which is made of bamboo or brass. When you flow out of this pipe, you are called Rum. You are no longer sweet Sugarcane, you make fools of wise people. I cannot befriend you.'

No other words were spoken. All had been said.

5   How thunder and lightning were made

ONCE UPON A TIME there lived a beautiful girl. She had long dark hair, her eyes sparkled with brightness and her skin glowed. All the boys in the village were in love with her. They desired to marry the girl. But whenever a boy approached her, she ran away as fast as she could. Whilst she ran she laughed. Even her laughter sounded warm and inviting, as if she begged the boy to pursue her. 'Come, follow me . . . ,' she seemed to call. But none of the boys ever reached her for she was very fast on her feet.

In this same village there lived a young man called Lakshman. He too adored the beautiful girl. He so wanted to marry her that he went to her father's house hoping that a marriage might be arranged. The father said: 'You must work in my house for twelve years. At the end of that time you may marry my daughter.'

Lakshman began the task which was demanded of him, for he loved the girl very much indeed. These were long years. When at last they had ended, he said: 'Master, twelve years have passed. You gave me your word. Please allow me to go home and let us be married as you agreed.'

When Lakshman had finished speaking, the man went into his house. He returned with a huge pot. The lid of the pot had been tightly sealed He said: 'Take this, my son. Carry the pot to your home. Under no circumstances open it before you get there. During the twelve years you were able to do as you were asked. This is the last occasion on which I request your obedience. I warn you not to open the pot until you arrive home. Your present will be there. I promise that all shall be well.'

Lakshman was happy to receive the pot. Even though it was heavy, he placed it on his head and began his journey. He walked alone. With every step he thought of the pot and wherever he looked he saw the pot's reflection. He so much wanted to look inside it. He knew he had been told not to open the lid, but he longed to see what the pot contained.

Struggling to obey the man's words he kept walking. Meanwhile the sun reached its highest point and with every step Lakshman felt the weight of the pot increase. How could it become heavier and heavier? What was inside it? He thought he heard a whisper. Had someone been put inside the pot? What if he was carrying the girl on his head? 'Do not open the pot till you reach home.' How he loathed those words. He tried being attentive to the road. He tried searching the sky with his eyes. He made so much effort to ignore the pot, that soon there was nothing else but the pot. He had to know what was inside it. His feet dragged wearily along the road. Did he hear laughter? The girl was laughing at him. He was certain he heard her laugh. 'I request your obedience.' Oh, but for a peep. One little peep could not make a real difference. She was laughing. He knew it for certain. The sweetness of her laughter made his heart beat very fast. He could no longer walk. Even though he was nearly home he had to stop. The pot was put down.

He could not resist any longer. The pot had to be opened. 'Just one quick look . . . ' Carefully he broke the seal and before he knew what had hit him, he saw his golden beloved shoot upwards into the sky. She flew away, shining so brightly. She ran across the clouds far beyond his reach.

'Don't go . . . ' he cried, 'Don't leave me.' He saw her sparkle in the far distant sky. In desperation he took his arrows and shot at her. He wanted her to come back to earth. He needed her beside him. His arrows crashed against the sky. She merely laughed. It was as if he saw her shining white teeth. Again she called, 'Come, follow me.'

Lakshman never left that place. He still sends arrows towards his beloved whenever he sees her. On a stormy night the people say: 'Can you hear the crashing of Lakshman's arrows? This is the thunder. Do you see the bright line that runs through the clouds? She is the beautiful girl who was never caught.'

6   *The magic pear tree*

A LONG TIME AGO in ancient China a farmer went to market. He had luscious pears to sell and was determined to ask a very high price. Once he had found a good place in the market, he cried out: 'Pears, beautiful pears . . . ' Whilst he was calling attention to his goods an old, ragged-looking monk came up to him. He humbly asked to be given one of the pears. The farmer, who was a mean, sharp person, said: 'Why should I give a pear to you? You're as lazy as anything and haven't done an honest day's work in your life.' As the priest did not walk away when insulted, the farmer became even more angry. He called him the nastiest things under the sun.

'Good sir,' said the monk, 'I cannot count the number of pears in your wheelbarrow. You have hundreds of them. I have only asked for one pear. Why has this made you so angry?'

By then a large crowd of people had assembled around the farmer and the poor monk. 'Give him a little pear,' someone suggested, in the hope that this might solve the problem. 'Do as the old man asks, for heaven's sake it is only a pear,' another one remarked, but the farmer would not hear of it. 'No is no is no,' he said. Finally a kind man bought one of the pears and handed it reverently to the old monk.

The monk bowed, thanked the kind man and said: 'You know that I am a holy man. When I became a monk I gave up everything. I have no home, no children, no clothes which I may call my own, no food other than what is given to me. How can you refuse to give me a single pear when I ask for it? I shall not be this selfish. I invite every one of you to eat one of the pears that I have grown. It shall be an honour if you accept my invitation.'

The people were startled. Why had he asked for a pear if he had so many pears with him. He did not seem to carry anything. What did the old man mean?

The monk ate his pear with great concentration until there was just one little pip left. He quickly dug a hole in the ground, planted the pip and covered it with earth. Then he asked for some water. One

of the people in the crowd handed him a cup. Hardly any time had passed when the bystanders saw how some green leaves had sprouted from the earth. These leaves grew very quickly. The people were astounded. In front of their eyes stood a small pear tree with branches and more branches and leaves, more and more leaves. Where the old monk had planted the little pip only minutes ago, there was a small pear tree. It grew faster and faster. They could see it grow.

Silence fell in the marketplace as the tree burst into flower and the flowers turned into large, sweet-smelling pears. The monk's face was aglow with pleasure. He picked the pears one by one and handed them to the crowd which had gathered to witness the miraculous growth of the pear tree. He handed them out until every one had been refreshed by a delicious pear. Then the monk took his axe and before the people even realised what was happening, the tree had been cut down. The monk simply picked the tree up, put it over his shoulder and went on his way.

The farmer had watched the scene in amazement. He had not been able to believe his eyes when the pear tree had grown out of the ground near his very own wheelbarrow which was full of pears. He looked at the barrow.

It was empty. Not a single pear was left in it. One of the handles of the barrow was missing too. Then the farmer knew what had happened. The old monk had used it to create the wonderful pear tree.

Of course the monk was nowhere to be seen. The tree which the monk had picked up with such great ease was found a little further down the road. It was the missing handle from the wheelbarrow. The farmer was in a towering rage, whilst the onlookers laughed.

Working with the stories

When Hare heard of Death

BEYOND THE BARRIERS OF ISOLATION

Play 'Freeze tag'. Move in slow motion in a boundaried area. Once tagged, freeze in posture. The game continues until everyone has been frozen. Focus on what it feels like to be standing there, motionless. Then let go. (It is helpful to change the person who is 'it'. This can be done by giving 'it' the option either to tag another player or to pass on being 'it'.)

Move the invisible barrier. Find a place in the room where you can stand with ample space around you. Imagine that a comfortable distance from you there is an invisible barrier. You would like to move beyond it, but are prevented from doing so. Test its strength/height/width. There are players on the other side of the barrier. You want to join them, but have great difficulty doing so due to the barriers, which are everywhere. After some time and hard work you succeed in making contact.

Reflect on your experience.

Tell the story 'When Hare heard of Death'.

Recall the time when you first became aware that the people you love will one day die, and/or that you yourself will die. Allow yourself to recall this.

Give each group member as many sheets of newspaper (cut to A4 size) as there are group members as well as an equal number of sheets of A4 writing paper.

Each group member will have exactly two minutes to share their experience. This time can be used to talk or to remain silent, or to do both. (N.B. Help group members to work within the time boundary as this is of crucial importance!)

RESPONSE TASK: after having listened to a group member, tear a small or a large hole in the sheet of newspaper. Place this on top of the writing paper. An irregular shape emerges. This is the outline of a brief poem. Write this poem. Let it reflect your response to the person's contribution, their silence and/or their words. (This may seem a difficult response task. It is surprisingly easy.)

Give the poems to each group member concerned.

Read the poems which were written for you.

Connect: make some connections between the poems, your earlier invisible barrier work and your first response to death as a reality.

Share some of your thoughts and feelings.

Reflect upon the entire session.

How the elephant died

IF ONLY . . .

Paint the image evoked by the word 'destroy'. Do not yet discuss your paintings.

Take a lump of modelling clay.

Tell the story 'How the elephant died'.

RESPONSE TASK: whilst listening to the story, use your clay to express your feelings. Put whatever you have modelled near your painting.

Remind yourself of the story and note those moments in the story where destruction or the wish for revenge and punishment gained hold.

Record these moments.

Ask yourself what might at each of these moments have stopped the events from unfolding in the way they did.

Write down which quality/characteristic would have been required to enable this to have happened. Begin your statements with 'If only . . . '. E.g. 'If only Hare had been well nourished.' 'If only the other elephants had been more observant.' 'If only the elephant had been aware of the weight of stones.'

Share your 'If only' statements with a partner.

Place your paintings and clay work inside the circle.

Select one of your 'If only' statements.

Change this statement from 'If only' into 'I want' (e.g. 'If only Hare had been well nourished' is changed into 'I want to be well nourished').

Reflect whether or not this change of statement is pertinent to your personal situation.

Talk about the implications of this alteration, your painting and the clay work.

Reflect upon the entire session.

Nyambe leaves the earth

IS WITHDRAWAL UNAVOIDABLE?

Through mime, create a small imaginary basket. It has a lid which can be lifted. Pass the basket around the circle. When you receive the basket, open it and look inside. It contains a small object. All you need to do is notice the object you see. Close the imaginary basket by putting the lid down. Pass it on to the person next to you. When the last person receives the basket, he/she looks inside it, closes it and magics it away.

Talk a little about the experience.

Remind yourself of something you have made. Maybe a picture, an item of clothing, a meal you have cooked or a photograph you took. Select one of these.

Talk to a partner about the process of 'making'. Share your experience. Try to focus on the beginning, middle and ending stages of the making process.

Return to the circle. Share some of your ideas.

Join groups of three: The person in the middle stands with arms outstretched, knees unlocked. Partners on either side pull the person gently first one way, then the other. (Take care to work slowly and carefully!) Switch places. Now work simultaneously around the theme of 'feeling pulled apart' without anyone actually pulling you.

Share your experiences.

Tell the story 'Nyambe leaves the earth'.

Write quickly a list of the kind of questions you would like to ask Nyambe.

Place a chair in front of the group. This chair will be used to 'hot-seat' Nyambe. Group members in turn will occupy the seat. A question will be asked. Each 'Nyambe' will answer one or two questions in substantial detail.

When you have heard the various questions and answers, recall one question which feels relevant to you and your current life situation. Record this question and formulate your own actual answer.

Share your writings with the group.

RESPONSE TASK: create a 'ponder' sheet. When someone has read their work, record which issue you would like to ponder for a while longer. For example, is withdrawal an advisable option? What about anger? You may find that you return to the same theme. That's fine.

Look at your various themes for pondering.

Share some of these.

Reflect upon the entire session.

The rice and the sugarcane
THEMES OF FRIENDSHIP

Recall something you noticed this morning, which you have not yet shared with anyone.

Describe this experience.

Share with a partner an event or memory of which you have been reminded whilst listening to the other group members.

Use finger paints to create a picture around the theme of friendship. Remind yourself of important friends. You may decide to use symbols to represent these friends. Make sure that you find a space/form for those people who have been/ are important to you.

Imagine that you can see your friendship with these people in bird's eye view. Witness the ups and downs of the relationships, the good and the troubled times.

Return to the circle.

Share your painting and some of your reflections with the group.

Tell the story 'The Rice and the Sugarcane'.

Imagine that Sugarcane has confided in you and told you about the day's events. When reflecting upon what she has told you, you decide to send her a letter of encouragement.

Write this letter.

Read your writings to the group.

RESPONSE TASK: each group member has as many small, colourful cards as there are group members. When a letter has been read, write/paint something on a card, which is a response to the letter you have just heard. When all members have read their letters, distribute the cards.

Look at the cards you have received.

Recall the session's work: what had been noticed this morning, the friendship painting, the story, the letters and the cards.

Select one statement or idea which you want to share with the group.

Reflect upon the entire session.

How thunder and lightning were made
WHEN CHANGE IS AVOIDED

Record words/sentences which spring to mind in response to 'You'll have to wait a long, long time.'

Share some of these.

Join groups of three or four.

Select some of the statements mentioned. Create and rehearse a brief enactment in which you make use of these sentences. Present your work to the group.

Discuss your experiences.

Explore as many different forms of running as is possible in the room you work in. For example: Running towards – to catch a train or to embrace a beloved. Running away from a pursuer. Explore your run in slow motion/at high speed.

Tell the story 'How thunder and lightning were made.'

Discuss which three major responses the villagers may have to Lakshman who still stands there, hoping to catch a glimpse of the girl he loves (e.g. admiration, irritation, indifference).

Join groups of three or four.

Discuss these responses. Then create a brief voice/choral-based improvisation. In this song/enactment the villagers address Lakshman. Imagine that the villagers really want him to be aware of what they think and feel.

Present your work and discuss your presentations.

Paint a picture of the way you feel right now. Which memories/associations does this evoke?

Share these with the group.

Think/speak of a minor change which might help you to feel greater strength, and mention what this change could be.

Reflect upon the entire session.

The magic pear tree

APPROPRIATE PUNISHMENT?

Sit in a circle. Eyes closed. An observer walks round the outside of the circle and gently taps one of you on the shoulder. This person will be the bestower of sleep. Sleep is bestowed by looking a group member in the eye and winking at them. You can avoid being winked to sleep by establishing eye contact with another group member. This eye contact can, however, only be held for a count of three. Then they must let go and search for someone else to look at. The game finishes when nearly everyone is asleep.

Rest with your eyes closed and breathe deeply. Then open your eyes.

Recall a situation in which you outwitted someone. If you have difficulty remembering such a situation, recall one where you were outwitted.

Share your memories.

RESPONSE TASK: whilst listening to the memories use finger paints to create an image evoked by the word 'triumphant'.

Tell the story 'The magic pear tree'.

Imagine that you are the duped farmer. Write a letter to the village council on behalf of the duped farmer, asking that something be done about this monk's many tricks.

Collect and re-distribute the letters.

Imagine that you have been part of a careful process of deliberation with the other village council members. You have come to a decision regarding the farmer's complaint/request.

Write a letter to the farmer stating the decision which the council members have reached and how this decision will be implemented.

Read both the letter you received and the response which you have written.

Look at your earlier painting.

Talk about your ideas/experiences with particular reference to punishment, banishment, treatment and forgiveness.

Reflect upon the entire session.

A few questions to explore

o How do hares live?

o In which ways do mountains crumble?

o What are igneous, metamorphic and sedimentary rocks?

o Why do elephants live in herds and what are the duties of the elephant leader?

o How does an African elephant warn its enemies?

o Why do animals and people attack each other?

o How do bees make honey?

o Why is the baboon a ground-dwelling creature? What kind of fighters are they when attacked?

o What is the function of blood and what are the dangers of great blood loss?

o What are the advantages of learning by imitation?

o What are the arguments for and against vegetarianism?

o Which methods do people use to kill animals?

o What are the actual layers of the earth's atmosphere?

o To which dangers is the atmosphere exposed?

o How are rice and sugar cane farmed?

o What are the advantages and disadvantages of intensive farming?

o What is alcohol and what is it used for?

o What is lightning?

o What is thunder?

o What characterises markets all over the world?

o What are fruits? Which function do they fulfill in a plant's life?

o How do seedlings germinate and grow?

o What is meant by 'hypnotic suggestion'? How does it work?

SIX

RETURN TO LIFE AGAIN?

From perfect grief there need not be
Wisdom or even memory!
One thing then learnt remains to me –
The woodspurge had a cup of three.
DANTE GABRIEL ROSSETTI

Change is happening all around us. Suddenly more quickly than we had anticipated. People are breaking away from what they call 'restricting situations'. Beards disappear, whilst others display a dramatic new hairstyle. It is both startling and somewhat alarming to notice how explicit group members desire to be in their declarations. The consequences of change must obviously be made clear. But this clear? Does it really matter that we express ourselves quite so publicly? The very conspicuousness of the arrival of newness arouses a degree of mistrust. Somewhere there has to be residual anxiety which is being ignored whilst the flag of innovation flies jubilantly. Who is doing the sacrificing? Where has the pain gone?

At this turning point in the group process the pain is likely to have become localised in one or two group members, whose adaptation to change is not leading to a sense of satisfaction, but instead has resulted in internal rupturous pain. Their pattern of functioning at an earlier time may have been troubled, now they are wounded. For these few members the problems which were uncovered during the process have been much greater than anticipated. Yet the discoveries were irreversible. What was known could not be unknown. With a heavy heart the right choices had to be made at the wrong time. This caused the wounding, evoking in its wake memories of other premature decisions. Memories too of earlier forced adaptation to change which one was not yet ready for. Consequently this particular process of change in the group, for which they had believed themselves to be sufficiently strong, has become extra painful and potentially devastating.

The cost is great, if not too great. Those who arrived at the blessed gate of the group's near-ending gladdened by their own success, have difficulty tolerating or even understanding the pain of those who did not make it in the same joyous way. Recalling memories of times when we were given our exam results and had failed, or the encounter with a broken-hearted friend whilst we ourselves were aglow with the fullness of love. The sudden momentum of our effort to change has caught most of us completely unaware. Stuckness became unstuck so rapidly. Most were able to enjoy the sudden freeing of energy. Some could not. Tossed about by the urgency of change, they lost more than they had bargained for, and now feel dishevelled. Shipwrecked on the shores of other group members' understanding, they may look for compassion and find little. The self-satisfaction of recent achievement tends to blind us.

Consequently the group faces once more the beguiling temptations of 'indifference', with which we struggled all along in its various disguises. We want to progress and help other people to enjoy the gains of our journey. We long to share our recently discovered new satisfactions, one of which relates to group cohesiveness and mutual support. Why then are some people testing these satisfactions to the utmost, dragging behind and hurting so much? Why cannot our enthusiasm infect them? The group wants to move forward with the swell of newly born energy. To safeguard the fruits of its labour. Are not these fruits in danger of being poisoned by the prolonged sorrow of some members who are simply mourning their necessary losses?

At this particular point in time, the group does not want to be confronted with self-doubt. Or with even more pain. It has been enough. It is intolerable to question the achievements. To explore the cost of change. Was it really too much for some of us? Our hair has already been cut. From now on it can only grow. The group resists regrets. Once caught in the whirlpool of change, it is probably less than considerate.

Do we really need to be reminded of our omissions and unkindness at this stage of our journey through change? If we want to be aware of what happens, we must. We need to ascertain the consequences for better and for worse of all that we invest in the process. Some people are still thoroughly disheartened. Angry even. It is tempting to ignore them and ride along on the wave of enthusiasm.

Whilst we are well nourished, others starve. Was not that realisation the inspiration for change in the very first place? The indifference needs to be taken on board. Otherwise our gains will be cancelled by our loss. Once more we turn to meet the sorrow and the pain which dwell within.

1 Mantis and the eland

M ANTIS, the Maker of Fire, finds Kwammang-a's shoe. His son's shoe. He picks it up, for he wants to make something. By the side of the pool, near the rushes, Mantis sits and thinks. Then he makes a new being, an eland-being. The eland hides amongst the rushes. Mantis names this one 'Kwammang-a's shoe's piece'. He cuts honey for the eland, and puts it near the water. He returns home.

Then, before the sun rises, he goes back to the pool. He calls: 'Kwammang-a's shoe's piece!' The eland comes from the reeds and walks towards his father. Mantis strokes him. He rubs his skin with honey, making the eland – whom he made from his son's shoe – look very beautiful.

Mantis goes to cut more honey, which he leaves with the eland. Then he returns home. Once more Mantis goes to the pool to call the eland-son whom he made from Kwammang-a's shoe's piece.

The eland stands shyly, whilst his father strokes him gently. And Mantis weeps, for he grows fond of him.

For three nights Mantis does not return, and for three nights the eland grows.

Again Mantis goes and calls Kwammang-a's shoe, the one he has grown fond of. He rubs his skin with honey. Then he goes home. The next morning he asks young Ich-neu-mon to come with him to the pool. Mantis speaks to Ich-neu-mon. He says 'Go sleep now,' but young Ich-neu-mon deceives him, and looks whilst Mantis caresses the eland.

Mantis knows Ich-neu-mon has seen Kwammang-a's shoe's piece, his eland-son. And he tells young Ich-neu-mon that it is but a very small thing. Something Ich-neu-mon's father Kwammang-a had dropped.

But young Ich-neu-mon tells his father Kwammang-a. And Kwammang-a is taken to see the eland. Mantis is not there then, he is in another place. Young Ich-neu-mon knows the call which Mantis used to see the eland. The eland, hearing his father's call, comes from the rushes. The people look at it.

Then Kwammang-a kills the eland. He cuts it up, while Mantis is not there.

When Mantis arrives, this is what he sees. He sees his people cutting the eland, the one he has made and rubbed to look beautiful. He says: 'I was not there. I was not with the eland when he died.'

He scolds his people. They have killed the eland, and they did this without him saying so.

Kwammang-a says, Mantis must gather wood, for this is meat and the people must eat.

But again Mantis says that if the eland had to be killed, he had wanted to tell them to do it. He had wanted to be there with the eland whom he himself made. Then his heart would not have been sore. Now there is nothing left but bones and gall. Mantis hurts. He is wounded. He says to himself that he will pierce the gall. The gall speaks, warning him that it will burst and blind him.

Mantis goes away to gather some wood. But again he returns to the place where the gall is. He says that he will pierce it open.

Young Ich-neu-mon and Kwammang-a know that Mantis must leave the place where the gall is. They ask him to go along homewards. But Mantis says that he must turn back. They try to say that 'no; they really must go home now.' But Mantis says that he must go back to the place where the eland was cut.

He returns. Then he pierces the gall.

It covers him. He can no longer see. Darkness is everywhere. He goes groping along. Groping, groping along. Groping along, until he finds an ostrich feather. A feather of the bird who gave him fire. Then he wipes the gall from his eyes with the feather. He throws it into the sky and says:

'You must now lie up in the sky. Be the moon, but grieve for the eland. You shine at night, and by your shining lighten the darkness for people till the sun rises to light up all things. It is he under whom we hunt; walk about, return home. But you are the moon; you give light to all people, then you fall way. You return to life again.'

This the moon does; it falls way and returns to life.

2   Tiger and Fox

IT HAPPENED A LONG TIME AGO. Maybe yesterday. Tiger had caught Fox. Fox said daringly: 'Tiger, if you devour me I will deeply respect your courage. Do not forget that the heavenly gods commended that I be the emperor of the animal world. You will go against their order if you eat me. Your courage will therefore have to be great. Though I shall be in the other world once you have eaten me, I shall offer my respects to you and bow to your greater might.'

Silence reigned. Fox resumed: 'Tiger, you do not believe me. You doubt the verity of my words and fail to be convinced. This is my challenge. I shall walk in front of you. You must follow immediately behind me. Then you will see with your own eyes that all the animals speed away as soon as they catch sight of me. The grace which the gods bestowed upon me frightens them.'

Tiger listened to Fox. Therefore he could not but accept the challenge. Nose to tail they walked through the forest. Fox had indeed spoken the truth. All the animals fled. Tiger's amazement was great. Puny Fox was indeed the emperor of the animal world. He elected not to challenge heaven's wisdom. Tiger went on his way.

3   Bat and his mother

B AT LIVED WITH HIS OLD MOTHER. Suddenly she became very ill. Bat called the antelope and said to him: 'Make my mother some medicine.' The antelope looked carefully at Bat's mother to see what ailed her. Then he said: 'Only the sun can help your mother,' and the antelope went away.

Early in the morning, Bat went to see the sun, but it was already eleven o'clock in the morning when they met. Bat said: 'I'm on my way to see you.'

The sun answered: 'If you have something to say, speak.'

Then Bat asked: 'Come with me, my mother is sick, make her some medicine.'

The sun answered and said that he could not make any medicine on the road and that Bat had to meet him in his own house. Therefore Bat had to come and see him early the next day.

Bat returned home. The day passed, night fell and everyone slept. Bat left home even earlier, but now it was nine o'clock when he met sun, and again sun said: 'Once I've left home, I do not go back. Come another day.'

Bat went back home, and so it happened that Bat travelled five more times to see sun, and every day he was late.

On the seventh day Bat's mother died. Bat was grief-stricken and said: 'If the sun had made some medicine, my mother would have recovered. The sun has killed her.'

Many people came to share Bat's mourning. They mourned the whole day. Then Bat ordered that his mother's body be carried to her grave. This happened. When they came to the grave, the beasts said that they always looked at a person's face before burial. They wanted to look upon Bat's mother too.

When they saw her, they said: 'No, we cannot bury her. She is not one of us. She is not a beast. She has a head like us, but she also has wings. Therefore she looks like a bird. Call upon the birds to bury her.' Thus they left.

Bat called the birds, and they came, all of them, and they too asked to see Bat's mother. Bat let her be seen. They looked very attentively. Then they spoke and said: 'Yes, she looks like us, for she has wings as we do. But we do not have teeth. None of us have teeth. She is not one of us, because she has teeth. She is not one of us.'

Much time passed as they talked. Meanwhile the ants came. They entered the body of Bat's mother. There was nothing he could do to drive them away. To make matters worse, one of the birds said: 'You should not have postponed the burial. I warned you that such a thing might happen.' The birds flew away.

Then all the birds and the beasts were gone.

Bat was all alone. He spoke to himself and said: 'I blame the sun for all my trouble. My mother would still be alive, if only he had made her some medicine. I shall never look upon the sun again. We shall never be friends. I shall hide myself when the sun shines forth. I shall neither greet him nor ever look at him.'

Then Bat spoke and said: 'I shall grieve for my mother for all time. I shall visit nobody. I shall always walk in darkness, lest I meet anyone.'

4 The origin of O-Pe-Che, the robin redbreast

THERE WAS A MAN who wished that his son would become a great hunter. His dreams for the boy's life were powerful. When the period of transition from boyhood to manhood arrived the man gave his child precise instructions about the manner in which he had to conduct himself during the time of fasting. He told the boy that if he were to fail to meet the trials with courage and determination, he would not be granted a strong guardian spirit. Then he could not be a great hunter.

A lodge was made ready for the boy. Inside water had been poured over hot stones. The air was saturated with dense steam. The boy entered. Here he cleansed himself, staying as long as was necessary. Then he plunged into the river. He repeated this process twice.

When the boy had been purified by water and heat, his father took him to another secret lodge deep in the forest. This lodge too had been built especially for the boy's journey. Inside it lay a beautiful mat which had been woven by the boy's mother. As soon as the boy lay down upon the mat, he dressed himself in silence. With the promise that he would return on the morning of each day of the boy's fast, the father bid his farewell.

The father did return every morning to speak words of encouragement to his child. He said that he was proud of the boy's willingness to endure his trials. The eighth day brought great sorrow. The boy was abandoned by his strength. His limbs stiffened. He could no longer move. Was he about to die?

When his father came on the morning of the ninth day, the boy said: 'My father, my dreams portend ill. I am visited by spirits who cast dark shadows upon the hopes which you have for me. Grant me permission to end this fast. Maybe another time will be better. I shall try again. My strength fails me utterly.' His father did not reply.

Once more the boy dressed his face in silence. He neither spoke nor moved till the eleventh day. Again he whispered his request. His father replied: 'Tomorrow I shall come early and bring you a little food.' With all strength drained the boy could only obey. He surrendered his whispering will and breathed imperceptibly. No longer did he note time's passing. Day made way for night and night for day, but he did not notice the change. He lay without motion whilst outside the lodge trees bent and whispered. Their branches softly groaning in the wind. The river ran from rock to rock. Here he had honoured the full strength of his boyhood and rejoiced in the emergence of manhood. In this place he lay with stiffened limbs far beyond the reach of thought.

The twelfth morning saw the father hurrying towards the lonesome lodge. He carried the promised food. When he came near the lodge, he heard a voice. He bent low and opened the peeping hole. Inside his son was sitting up, muttering to himself. He was painting his breast and shoulders wherever his hands could reach. He spoke barely audibly: 'My father killed me. He refused to hear me. I was obedient beyond my strength. My guardian spirit has come. He is not great. His heart is moved to pity. I shall be changed.'

The father pulled the lodge apart. He cried: 'My son! My son! Do not leave me.' Even as the old man pleaded with the boy not to die, the change occurred. He became a beautiful bird – the O-pe-che, the Robin Redbreast. Flying beyond his father's reach he spoke these final words:

'Do not mourn for me. I shall be happier this way. Never could I live your dreams. I would always have torn through your hopes. I could not be a great warrior. Now I shall cheer you with my song. The pains of humankind are mine no longer. Do not mourn for me.'

He spread his wings and hastened into the air.

The wise people say that O-pe-che kept his promise. He dwells close to our lodges and offers cheer.

5 The young man, the lion and the yellow flowered zwart-storm tree

A YOUNG MAN of the early race went hunting. He walked up a hill and looked around. Suddenly he became sleepy. He fell asleep by the side of a waterhole. What was happening?

A lion came to the waterhole. He was thirsty. Seeing the young man the lion gently lifted him up. The young man felt the lifting. He tried not to move, for he thought that the lion might bite and kill him. He did not move. Did the lion know that he was not dead?

The lion took the young man to the yellow flowered zwart-storm tree. He pressed the young man who felt sleepy firmly between the branches. His legs did not fit into the tree.

The lion had not drunk at the waterhole. He was thirsty and needed to soften his thirst before eating the young man. He took the young man's head and rested it on top of the branches of the yellow flowered zwart-storm tree. Then the lion returned to the waterhole.

The young man moved his head. He moved it a little. Looking back the lion noticed the movement. He was bewildered. He had stuck the young man in the tree. He had pressed him firmly between branches. The dead young man could not move.

When the young man fell out of the tree, the lion hastened back. He lifted him up and placed him firmly back into the tree. The young man's eyes filled with tears. The lion saw the tears and licked them away. The young man kept his eyes closed. He could feel the lion's gaze and held it steadily. Tears were flowing down his face and the lion licked them away. Again the lion pressed him firmly into the branches of the yellow flowered zwart-storm tree. He returned to the waterhole for he was still thirsty.

Suddenly the young man jumped from the tree. He ran this way. He ran that way. He knew the lion would pursue him. He did not go to his shelter.

When he saw the people of his village, he shouted that a lion had carried him. A lion had carried him! He asked to be rolled in hartebeest skins for he had been carried by a lion whilst the sun was high. He doubted not that the lion would follow his tracks. For such are the lion's ways.

Was he not their heart's young man? The villagers gathered the hartebeest skins. They did not want their heart's young man to be eaten by the lion. They did not want it. They rolled him in hartebeest skins and made him a hiding place. They covered him with skins and bushes for they loved him greatly.

An old bushman stood at the place where the young man had entered the village. He saw the lion in that place. He spoke and asked the early people to look at the one who appeared.

The young man's mother found strength. She spoke and said: 'Never can reason be found to let the lion enter our village. Shoot the lion before it trespasses into our shelter.'

The early people listened to her words. They took their quivers and faced the lion where it stood at the edge of the village. They shot it. Again and again they let their arrows fly. They could not kill the lion. A woman asked how come they shot, but could not kill the lion. An old man's voice was heard. He said: 'The lion will not die. The lion's will is with the young man he has carried.' He was their heart's young man. The people threw other children before the lion, but he touched them not.

The people tried to kill the lion. He was untouched. He kept his will with the young man. The people tried to spear him. They shot at him. The lion was not touched. He wanted the young man whose tears he had licked. He did not want another one, he wanted this young man whom he found by the waterhole.

The lion entered the shelters. He broke into them. The people again offered him another. But he would not eat this one. He wanted the young man whose tears he had licked.

The wise people spoke: 'The mother must be told to give her son to the lion who cannot be touched.'

The mother heard the people's words. She said: 'Be it so. But let him not be eaten. Let not the lion carry my son to an eating place. Let the lion die and lie with our heart's young man.'

The people took their heart's young man from the hiding place. They took away the hartebeest skins. They gave their young man to the lion. The lion came toward him, lifted him up and killed him.

The people stabbed the lion with their spears. Their spears entered him.

Then the lion spoke. He said: 'Now I can die. I have been given the young man whom I lifted and carried to the yellow flowered zwart-storm tree. I put him there and licked his tears. I sought him all this time. Now I lie with him. For I am his.'

The lion died. They both lay there dead, the young man and the lion. They were at peace and so were the people.

6   Bird-dreaming

IN THE DREAMTIME there were two men. By chance they came across each other in the middle of the forest. Both men had been walking for a long, long time. First they performed their ritual greetings, then they made the other one welcome. When they had done this they were ready to talk about their journeys. The first man spoke and said: 'I am looking for the roots of lilies. I therefore want to learn to fly.' The other man also spoke, saying: 'I am in search of fish. Therefore I too want to be able to fly.' They then looked at each other and they knew what they both wanted.

They spoke about their heart's desire and decided that they needed feathers. The one who was looking for fish wanted to have white feathers and green and black stripes on his back. He described how he could see the little deep-blue feathers of his bird's head and the red legs. Then he began to dance. His dance called forth his bird-dreaming song. It sounded like 'clack-clack-clack-a-clack.' He danced and danced and sang his song until his body grew the feathers he so wanted, until he became the bird he longed to be. He walked like a bird. He moved his arms for they were wings. He did move his arms like wings and flew away into the sky. Then he landed on the branch of a nearby tree. Perched on the branch of this tree he saw his friend standing in the middle of the forest, the man who was in search of lilies. The bird with the white feathers, the deep-blue head and the red legs, stretched his wings and returned to the meeting place in the depth of the forest.

Now the lily-seeker had discovered how he too might make feathers. He thought of himself as a bird with blue-grey feathers, a bright grey chest, red at the back of his head and yellow legs.

Then this one too began to dance. It was a different dreamtime dance and another dreamtime song. He moved with short, quick steps. He danced his bird-dreaming song-dance until he too could fly. It was not very gracious. He said that he still wanted to go and seek lily-roots. He is the Brolga crane. The other one still wanted to eat fish. He is the Jabiru heron.

This happened in the dreamtime and to this day the songs are heard. At special times the people sing the song of the Jabiru heron. Whenever the dreamtime is nearly forgotten the Jabiru heron sings his dreamtime song.

> Kaatchirook kaleenee
> Kaatchirook kaleenee
> Arkanar wurukee
> Kaatchirook wurukee
> Kaat.

Some people hear its call.

Working with the stories

Mantis and the eland

TAKING AND MAKING

Place a very smooth ball of modelling clay 25 cm in diameter in the centre of the circle.

Look carefully at this smooth ball of clay. Breathe quietly.

Take one by one a handful of clay. Witness the taking-away process and the feelings it evokes.

Make a ball out of your own piece of clay. Hold this ball in the palm of your hand. Look at it carefully. Then quickly make something out of this ball of clay. Place whatever you have made in front of you on a white sheet of paper.

Place a new ball of clay in the centre of the circle. Each group member takes another lump of clay.

Tell the story of 'Mantis and the Eland'.

RESPONSE TASK: as you listen to this story, make something out of the second piece of clay. When the story is finished, stop modelling. Place this sculpture near the previous one.

Walk around the room. Look at everyone's sculptures. Take several pieces of paper and a pen with you. When you look at a sculpture, think of a name you might give it. Leave this name by the side of each sculpture. Examples might be 'Protest', 'Agony', 'Contentment'.

Return to the circle.

In pairs look at the names which your sculptures were given. Then talk with your partner about the sculptures and about the feelings which the names evoke in you. Reflect on the way these relate to your current life-experience.

Return to the circle.

Share some of your thoughts, experiences and feelings with the group,

Reflect upon the entire session.

Tiger and Fox

NOT INTIMIDATED AND BOASTING NONETHELESS

Recall a memory of a time when you did not feel intimidated, even though you had every reason to feel so.

Share the memories.

RESPONSE TASK: listen to the memory and encapsulate this person's experience in one word. Write this word down.

Together select one word from those you have recorded.

Stand in a circle, clapping. Establish a group rhythm.

In turn each group member will enter the circle and offer a brief movement, improvisation or dance which embodies an aspect of the word which has been chosen. This word can also be used for vocal accompaniment. When the dance is complete the dancer returns to the circle. Another member goes into the circle.

Talk a little about the experience.

Tell the story 'Tiger and Fox'.

Imagine that one evening there is a gathering of foxes, all pretty smart like the one in the story. They meet in a circle and enter it to boast of their audacious tricks. They know that it is dangerous for foxes to be caught out using their boasting movements/sounds on their own. They must get the other foxes to copy their movements/sounds as soon as possible. Thus, the group of foxes learns about the boaster's deeds. They also dance their dances.

Reflect on your experience.

Ponder what kind of response might have been helpful to a person who had not been intimidated when threatened and who, nonetheless later, boasted.

Reflect upon the entire session.

Bat and his mother

NOTHING WILL EVER CHANGE?

In turn, the whole group *gently* whispers each member's first name. As if calling this person into the group. The person listens quietly. The experience can be intensified by closing your eyes.

Talk a little about this experience.

Whisper as in Chinese whispers, into a group member's ear: 'Nothing will ever change . . . ' The statement is whispered to the next person, and the next. Work with great concentration. Go round the circle several times.

Stand in a circle and speak with force these very same words. Explore the different levels of feeling which are evoked by the words.

Tell the story of 'Bat and his Mother'.

Join groups of three or four.

Explore how Bat could have been helped to become less pained/angry. First share some ideas. Then try out these ideas through dramatic/movement improvisation. Take turns in playing the part of Bat.

Create an improvisation which you can share with the rest of the group.

Present your work.

Reflect on the feelings evoked in you. Which situations or experiences have come back to mind?

Talk with a partner about these memories and feelings.

Share some of these with the group.

Paint the images of both hopelessness and hopefulness.

Share your paintings.

Reflect upon the entire session.

The origin of O-Pe-Che

TOO MUCH TOO SOON

Play a regular game of 'Tag' in an area which has been cleared of objects. When group members are energetically involved, suggest that at the moment of being tagged, he/she jumps into the air and briefly shouts as loudly as they wish to release some tension.

Stand in a circle holding hands. Two group members release contact and create a group-knot by intersecting, reversing direction, etc. When the group is unable to move any further, freeze. Feel the tension in your body. Intensify/then reduce the tension. Untie the knot. Reform the circle. Stand. Breathe. Release hand contact and rest.

Paint an image of the way you are feeling.

Tell the story 'The Origin of O-Pe-Che'.

Paint an image of how you are feeling now that you have heard the story.

Place both paintings near one another somewhere in the room.

Write an imaginary entry in a diary kept by a wise person who witnessed the development of the relationship between the father and his son. Describe in the diary entry how this person felt. Why she or he felt unable to intervene. How does this person respond to the boy's death? Begin your writings with the words: 'I am called . . . (name), the wise one . . . '

Share your writings.

RESPONSE TASK: listen to the diary-notes and ponder what this wise person could learn. What might comfort the wise one in these troubled times. Record your response.

Give your response to each reader.

Read what you have received. Collect your paintings and select one of the responses which connects with the way you felt during the making of the paintings.

Share this with the group.

Reflect upon the entire session.

The young man, the lion and the yellow flowered zwart-storm tree

CONSOLATION

Group sits or stands in a circle. A small ball is thrown from one group member to another. As you throw the ball, complete the sentence: 'I am . . . ' Add whatever comes to mind.

Paint the image evoked by the words 'The Untold'.

Look at all the paintings.

Leave a word-association near each painting.

Return to your own painting. Collect and read the words which were left.

Select three words which speak to you. You may not know why, but they resonate with you.

Write these words on another sheet of paper and connect each one with an as yet untold/unspoken event or longing in your life. Write about these.

Share your writings with each other.

RESPONSE TASK: when a group member has finished reading, ponder what you appreciate about having heard the experience/longing. Write this on a small piece of paper. Note: do not yet distribute these writings.

Tell the story 'The young man, the lion and the yellow flowered zwart-storm tree'.

Distribute and read the responses and select one or two which feel pertinent.

Use these words/this word to create a painting or to write about consolation. Consolation for all those who witnessed what happened.

Share your paintings or writings.

Connect: make connections between your own untold life events and longings, the story and your paintings.

Reflect upon the entire session.

Bird-dreaming

WANTING VERY MUCH INDEED

Paint a picture which represents what it feels like to want something just a little, a little more, and even more, and very, very much indeed.

Recall a time when you wanted something badly. What was it you wanted?

Write about your experience.

Share your paintings and writings with the group.

Tell the story 'Bird-dreaming'.

Reflect on what was lost in the process of transformation and equally on what was gained.

Share your ideas/concerns with a partner and select several which are important for both of you.

Use these ideas to work through movement to find a physical form for your thoughts. Allow yourself to be surprised by the way in which the work develops.

Discuss which elements of your movement-work can be used to create a brief presentation to the group. Rehearse your presentation.

Share your work.

RESPONSE TASK: when watching the work, ask yourself what each of the dancers might really want/desire. Create a small gift representing your interpretation of this wish/desire.

Share your gifts.

Look at what you have received and select one or two which feel pertinent.

Reflect upon the entire session.

A few questions to explore

○ What is special about the praying mantis?

○ What are the three castes in a honey bee society?

○ How do bees build their hives?

○ What is gall and what is its function?

○ Explore the differences in the life spans of living beings.

○ Why do animals in the wild have shorter life spans?

○ What is hunger? When does it become starvation?

○ What are the dangers of starvation? How can they be remedied?

○ How many people in our world are starving? How many die from starvation or from disease linked to starvation every day?

○ Why are foxes often considered to be cunning?

○ What is meant by animal hierarchy?

○ Why do tigers have stripes?

○ What is special about bats?

○ Why can most species of bat fly in complete darkness?

○ What happens to a dead animal's body when left in the wild?

○ What are rites of initiation?

o Explore different ways of weaving.

o Design some dwelling-places made of sticks or poles or leaves or hides.

o How do birds choose a territory?

o Why do robins sing?

o Why do lions often lie in wait at a waterhole?

o How do female lions hunt and why do male lions usually not hunt?

o Why is it unusual for a lion to face a human being?

o How is it possible for birds to fly?

o Describe some bird courtship displays.

SEVEN

TO BUILD A NEW VILLAGE

For thou art with me, here, upon the banks
of this fair river; thou, my dearest Friend,
my dear, dear Friend, and in thy voice I catch
the language of my former heart . . .
WILLIAM WORDSWORTH

Many are the reasons why we cry for a vision. Withdrawing into solitude or seeking our inspiration amidst the crowds of inner cities, we lament in the hope of finding something that remains. Maybe a lasting comfort, maybe a replenishing source of joy. Maybe simply to have the strength to endure the full impact of reality.

Some of these experiences we share. Others hesitate within us, becoming shy before the fixity of language. We have gone through a process of change and discovered the nature of the process. This may have been an unexpected bonus. When next we are out of tune, we have internalised a way of approaching our complexities.

We are aware that it matters to know about the anticipated length of a process of change and consequently of the likely commitment which is required. We have experienced the power of the tidal 'move away – draw closer' dynamic, having learned through tough experience how to come to grips with some of these. We were compelled to take stock of our actual and imagined resources. Now we understand more clearly the many ways in which we block ourselves and others from making the best use of these.

When, during the closing stages of the group, we turn to meet once more the sorrow and pain which dwell within, we discover somewhat to our surprise our own unmourned losses. Feelings about the ending of this project, this group, which we had tried to push away. Because they feel too uncomfortable and anyway that is how we are used to handling good-byes. Cheerfully not tearfully.

Once we acknowledge that we are about to go our different ways, that imminent separation is a reality, we are able to address our feelings. To our surprise there are some outstanding issues which we would like to settle. We mention the strange, somewhat guilty feelings which are attached to something that occurred awhile ago. The other person initially says that he or she cannot recall quite what happened. We speak a little about it. They respond: 'Oh yes. Indeed. No. Yes. You are right. I didn't like that. True, I did avoid you for a while after that incident. That you remember it . . . Well, thanks for the apology.' The smile, and the quality of the look which we later receive, suggest that something has been repaired. That it mattered to say sorry beyond the initial easy-going denial.

We try to visualise what it will be like not to have the structure and the expectations of the group to facilitate our encounter. We may never see these people again. Fantasies about who shall stay in touch with whom emerge. Some of these are based on the reality of developed friendships. Others are the playing of a hunch. Especially because we may never meet again, we need to acknowledge the bonds which exist between us. Which roads are these people, with whom we have shared such a lot, about to travel?

We become acutely aware of the sense that we are like fellow travellers about to embark on different routes, knowing that for quite some time we walked kindred paths. Maybe our roads will cross again. Maybe not. We want to make sure that all of us are as well prepared as we can be for the journey which lies ahead. We want to bestow some care and blessings. We would like to receive such blessings too. Bowing our heads over the uncertain map of life anticipated, we try to point out tricky bridges and dangerous slopes which have to be traversed. We also assure ourselves that our companion knows how to seek help when necessary. How to discern approaching danger.

This is the time of slow parting. We try to give each other the attention we deserve. When all is said and done, we rest together for a little while. The silence which now falls is no longer poignant with the unspoken. All has been said. Completeness dwells within. The group is truly ready to say good-bye. Then we let one another go, not prematurely and with a heavy heart. But securely and with good faith that we travel our roads each to the best of our ability. If the desire to meet again were to grow strong and if the wish were to be mutual, then it only takes two people to arrange an encounter. We realise this. Maybe life itself will provide an unexpected occasion. Who knows. It does not matter at this moment. With such hope and inspired by new visions, we accept that permanent change-ability is all that is required of us.

This much we have gained. We go our very own way.

1 *Once more Sinaa moved*

I N THAT TIME, when the rain began to fall, the Juruna Indians had everything. Sinaa, the one-with-eyes-in-his-back, told the Juruna that the rivers were rising and that soon the forests would be hidden underneath the water. Even the hills would disappear beneath the water. He told them: 'Let us make a very big canoe and plant our food inside it.' Sinaa carved the canoe. It was a huge canoe, which could offer space to many people. Part of the canoe was filled with earth. In this part he planted manioc, corn, potatoes and other herbs and shrubs. This garden grew quickly and renewed itself each day.

The rivers rose. As Sinaa had said, everything became water. The animals had to swim. The tapirs and the pigs, they too tried to swim, but they drowned. The birds flew above the water. They could not find land either. Sinaa and his people entered the canoe. They went from here to there. Some people fled to high hill-tops. They did not have food. Sinaa gave food to these people. Though some turned away. They got lost and became wild. Sinaa pleaded with his people not to wander. To stay near one another. He warned his people about getting lost.

At last the rains stopped. Sinaa then searched for the people who had wandered. They had gone beyond the place where he could have found them. They had not believed his words. When the rains stopped, Sinaa spoke, saying: 'The land will become dry. Do not stray. Keep by my side. Those who go looking for land will surely get lost.'

The boat and the water sank together. Sinaa remembered where the main valley and the river were. He knew their whereabouts. The people kept asking: 'Where is the river?' He answered that it was still a long way away. They asked again and he said that they were nearly there. The tree tops were showing themselves. The canoe followed the tree tops and at last Sinaa said: 'This is our river.'

Those who had remained in the hills came down later. They came down when the land was dry. They were confused and did not stay long in the presence of the others. They left and became wild people.

This was the time of separation. Each group received a different language. Sinaa also took some string. He cut the string into pieces and gave part of it to each group. Then Sinaa and his people continued their journey. They travelled down river. It was a long journey. When they arrived in the place of homecoming, they built a village. More and more people were born. They became many.

In those days the Juruna ate human flesh. It was the flesh of other Indians whom they had killed. At a certain time Sinaa told his granddaughter to get him some meat which was being roasted next door. She asked, but was not given food. Sinaa told her to go again. He was sure that they would give her meat this time.

They did not. They pulled the little girl towards themselves and raped her. She cried when she came back to Sinaa, who had knowledge of their deed. Sinaa could not stay in that place. It was a place of upset.

When the people saw that Sinaa was making ready to leave, they wanted to kill him. They wanted to kill their chief. They followed him with arrows and shot at him and his family, but none of them were hurt for Sinaa had closed their bodies against the arrows, though they were bruised. His sons wanted to fight their followers. Sinaa did not want this. He frightened the people who were shooting arrows. They went away. Sinaa and his family travelled for many days until they came to a place where they built a new village.

The people followed them to this place. They were curious how Sinaa had sealed his family's bodies. Sinaa showed them how men can make their bodies hard by not sleeping with women. The next day Sinaa tested the men by shooting at their chest. One man died and became a stone, which still stands in that place.

Time passed. Again Sinaa travelled down river. He built a new village. The Juruna who had hardened their bodies joined him there. Some people from the previous village also came. This was a little later. But Sinaa moved again. He only took his own people. Again some others followed. It was that way.

Once more Sinaa moved. Now they were near the big water. Then all of Sinaa's people, all of them, joined him there. Sinaa offered to make them any present they wanted. He made many necklaces. Then some Juruna returned to their previous villages. Others stayed. The ones who left began using a different language.

These people visited again after some time, but no one understood them then. Because they were not understood they went back. They came across another people. Again they asked for what they wanted. Again they were not understood. They shot arrows at the people who had not understood them. Since that time they take by force what they want and need. They no longer ask. They are not understood.

Sinaa goes on living in that place. A Juruna Indian visited him there. Sinaa had married an enormous spider who wove clothing. Sinaa was old and white with age, but whenever he took a bath, he would become young again. He could rejuvenate because he was able to pull his old skin off over his head, like taking off an old sack. Sinaa asked after his people. He asked how they were. Then he took the Juruna Indian to see a tall forked stick. Sinaa told him that the stick supports the sky. Pointing at the stick he said: 'When the last of our people dies, I shall pull the stick down. When this happens the sky will fold. Because the stick has gone it collapses. Then all the people will die. They will disappear. The day that I remove the stick will be the end of everything.'

2 *The four friends*

RAVEN, Rat and Tortoise were talking with each other by the side of a beautiful fountain when a small wild goat came running towards them. She ran with great fear. Raven, Tortoise and Rat immediately understood that a great hunter must be chasing her. They swiftly moved away to look after themselves. Tortoise hid in some nearby water, Rat hurried into a neat little hole and Raven flew to the top of the tree which stood by the side of the fountain.

The little wild goat stopped and even though the water in the fountain was clear, she did not drink. Raven called Tortoise and when Tortoise saw that the little goat was thirsty but not drinking, he said: 'Drink, little Goat, the water is clear. And then please tell us why you were running with such great fear.'

At that point Rat came out of her hole and Raven flew down from the tree. When the friends had gathered Goat told the three animals that, as they had guessed, she had nearly been caught by a great hunter. The animals were well pleased that she had escaped and asked her to stay with them. She would be quite safe in their company. They could now be four friends instead of three – and so it was.

The four friends lived happily together. Then one day Goat did not come to their meeting place at the fountain as was usual. Raven, Rat and Tortoise waited a long time. They missed her and wondered what had happened. At last they decided that they would search for their friend.

Raven flew high into the sky. He looked everywhere until he saw how Goat had been caught in a hunter's net. Tortoise and Rat were anxiously awaiting his return. When Raven folded his wings they knew that he brought sad news. Raven told them that he had seen how Goat was caught in a hunter's net. The three friends wondered what to do. Of course they had to rescue their friend. But how?

After a great deal of thought Raven spoke. He said to Rat: 'You can do it. You know how to free Goat. Do it quickly or the huntsman will kill her.' Rat agreed. She asked Raven to carry her in his bill as swiftly as he could to the place where Goat now lay. Then Rat would bite through the net's twine and Goat would be freed.

They agreed to Rat's plan. Raven took her into his beak and off they flew. Goat was very glad to see her friends. Rat gnawed through the twine as fast as she could. Meanwhile Tortoise travelled along the road to the place where Goat lay. He arrived just when Goat was freed.

Upon seeing Tortoise Goat cried: 'Oh no! Now the hunter will catch you. You're slow, Tortoise. None of us can carry you. I can run fast, Raven can fly and Rat can hide in a hole, but where can you go? There is no water near here.' Just then the hunter arrived. Little Goat ran away, and Raven flew high into the sky and Rat scurried into a hole, but as Goat had said, Tortoise had nowhere to go.

When the hunter saw that Goat had escaped, he looked everywhere. Goat was not to be seen. Then his eye spotted Tortoise, who was a big, big Tortoise. The hunter could not believe his luck. It was so easy to capture him. He was put in the same old net which only a little earlier had been round Goat. The Hunter lifted the net on to his shoulder and began the journey home.

As soon as he was on his way, the three friends dared to come out of their hiding places. They were angry that Tortoise had been caught. They were also very sad. Then Raven spoke, saying: 'We must save him.'

He had hardly finished speaking when Rat spoke. She said: 'We'll follow the hunter. Then Goat will run in front of the hunter and tease him into catching her. He cannot run after her with the net on his back. He'll have to put the net down.'

Goat liked Rat's plan. She said: 'I'll limp as if I'm hurt. That will surely make him think that he can catch me. Rat, you must then free Tortoise from the net like you freed me.'

They all agreed and went on their way. When the hunter saw Goat he did of course think that he could easily catch her now that she was limping so badly. He put the net down and chased the little wild Goat. Goat was very clever and led him a long way away. The chase was in vain. Dispirited the hunter returned to the net thinking that at least he still had a big, fat Tortoise. But by the time he returned to the net Tortoise was gone. Rat had gnawed through the strings and freed her friend. Suddenly the hunter was very frightened. How come that one who could run so fast as well as one who was so slow had escaped from his net? The place was haunted. It had to be haunted. Though really tired, he ran home as fast as he could.

Once more the four friends came out of their hiding places. Their friendship lasted till they died.

3 Was it not an illusion?

NOTHING EXISTED in the beginning. The Father reached towards an illusion. He encountered mystery. Nothing existed in the beginning. The Father Nai-mu-ena absorbed the dream, and thus dreaming he merged with thought.

Nothing was. How to support his dreaming? He spun the dream to a thread and held it. He was the dream's breath containing the emptiness, the illusion. He sought to reach for its base. He felt for its base. Nothing existed in the beginning.

Again the Father sought to reach the base of his dreaming. He encountered mystery. He thought the word 'earth'. The Father was one with the void and gathered it into his hands. Then he wove the dream-thread into the dream. He intertwined them with gum, joining the dream-thread and the dream with the magical gum, Iseike.

Then he seized the illusion, the base, and he trod upon it. He trod upon it repeatedly. Thus he seized the earth and flattened it. He flattened the dream earth.

Holding the dream, he let spittle flow and more spittle and more spittle. He let it flow from his mouth. Upon this flattened, illusory earth, he fastened the roof of the sky. He grasped his dream and made the blue sky and the white sky.

The maker of narratives sits where the sky meets the underworld. Thus the permission for this story's emergence was given. It was in our being when we were made.

4 The woodcutter and the king of the mice

T HE KING OF THE MICE lived in the roots of a banyan tree which stood in the middle of a dense forest. Near the forest lived two brothers. They were very poor. The younger one was a woodcutter. One day, when he had gone into the forest to work, the woodcutter's eyes fell upon the banyan tree. He thought to himself: 'If I cut that tree I could sell the wood in town and earn some money.' The king of the mice heard him think and became very worried. He rushed towards the woodcutter and said: 'Please, don't cut the tree down. It is my home. If you leave it standing you can visit me every evening and each time I shall give you a gold coin.'

The woodcutter was enchanted by the prospect of a piece of gold and promised that he would leave the tree alone. That evening he returned to the forest and as the king of the mice had foretold there was indeed one gold piece lying at the foot of the tree. The next night too the woodcutter returned and again he was given a piece of gold and the same thing happened the third evening. When he had received three gold pieces the woodcutter showed them to his brother, who could not understand what had happened. His younger brother had acquired three pieces of gold?

He asked him where he had found the gold or who had given it to him, but he did not get an answer. He was simply told: 'Don't ask me about it. Enjoy that it is ours.' But he became more and more curious, even angry. After all he was the elder of the two. He had a right to know where the gold had been found or what kind of feats his young brother had performed for which he had been so richly rewarded. At last he threatened him, saying: 'If you don't speak the truth, I shall tell everyone that you are a thief.'

The woodcutter was frightened of his older brother. Especially when he was angry. He decided to tell him everything. How he had seen the banyan tree. How the king of the mice had pleaded with him not to cut the tree down; how he even told him that if he were to visit the tree at night he would be given a piece of gold. The woodcutter said to his brother: 'Believe me or not, the king of the mice leaves the coins for me near the roots of the great banyan tree.'

'You are thick,' said his brother. 'You believe a little mouse. Of course there is a whole pot of gold underneath that tree. That is where he gets your gold pieces. You must get that tree out of the way. Cut it down and you'll see for yourself. There is gold between those roots. You're stupid waiting for the pieces one by one. Listening to a mouse . . .'

The next day the woodcutter went into the forest and he cut down the banyan tree. The king of the mice did not speak to him. There was no gold between the roots of the tree. Nor did he meet the king of the mice that time.

However, when evening came a mouse crept into the woodcutter's home. The gold pieces disappeared. The two brothers were as poor as they always had been.

5   How wisdom came among the tribe

THERE, in that place, Kwaku Ananse the Spider brushed together all the knowledge. He swept it to one spot. Then he took a gourd and put the knowledge into it. He closed the gourd tightly. Then Kwaku Ananse spoke. He said that he was taking the gourd with him. He would climb a high tree, the highest one he could find. He was going to hang the gourd in the top of that tree. No knowledge would be left on earth. No wisdom either. It would all be finished.

He did as he had spoken. He took that gourd with him. When he arrived by the highest of the high trees he took a piece of string. He tied it to the gourd which swung down in front of him and he made ready to climb that tree. He climbed and he climbed. It was no good.

In that place his young son, Ntikuma, stood. He watched his father trying to climb the tree with the gourd hanging down there in front of him. The son said: 'Your eyes must be turning away with shame. Shouldn't the gourd be on your back? Would you not be able to climb the tree with the gourd on your back?'

Spider said: 'Go away you child of old knowing.'

He clung to the tree and tried again to climb it. It was no better than before. He could not do it.

Kwaku Ananse thought a long time. Then he put the gourd on his back. He got climbing. He went quickly: up, up, up, he goes.

He came to the place where the branches stretch away from the trunk. Here he spoke and said: 'Listen. I, Kwaku Ananse, by the lesser God Afio! I am dying of shame. I'm dead already. My son is small, tiny, little. I stood there. I had gathered all the knowledge and the last morsel of wisdom. But I must have overlooked one little bit. My son, the one who still suckles, he was the one who showed it to me.'

There, where the branches meet the tree trunk, he took that gourd. He tore it open: *tintini*! Then he threw it away. There was a scattering, a sound of flying, *tesee*!

Because of this everyone got wisdom; some may not have got there in time. Do excuse me, but if that's you, well, you must be a fool.

6   Grandmother Spider brings the light

IN THE BEGINNING there was only darkness. The early people bumped into each other. They never saw anything, always groping about in blindness. Then they said to each other: 'We need light.' Woodpecker knew that there was light on the other side of the world. Fox warned that the people who had plenty of light were greedy, otherwise they would have shared the light before now. Woodpecker agreed but he nonetheless wanted to ask for some. Fox argued that they had to steal a tiny bit of light. The council of the early people wondered what to do.

Then Possum spoke. Pointing at his tail, he said: 'I have a thick bushy tail. I could hide the light inside my fur.' Possum set out. It was a long way to the other side of the world, and as the light grew brighter Possum screwed up his eyes. That's why his eyes are small even today, because of what he did for the early people. Though he had to screw up his eyes Possum kept going. He went all the way. When he found the sun, he snatched a tiny piece and stuffed it into his tail. His tail got badly burned for the sun was hot. You notice that Possum's tail is bald. That's why.

Then Buzzard went to steal the light. He thought he was wiser than Possum. When he had snatched a tiny piece of the sun, he put it on top of his head. His head feathers got burned. Which is why Buzzard is baldheaded.

The early people did not know what to do next. Possum and Buzzard had done their best. They were moaning to each other when a voice said: 'Let me try.' She had spoken very gently. It took a while before the others listened to Grandmother Spider, for it was her voice the people could not hear.

She said again: 'Let me try.' They let her. Feeling about in that great darkness, Grandmother Spider searched until she found some damp clay. She made a thick-walled pot. It was a small one. She started eastwards, the same as Possum and Buzzard, but she spun a thread behind her so that she knew the way home.

No one even saw her when she came close to the sun. She was so small. She reached out one of her hands and gently took a small bit of sun and put it in the bowl. Holding the bowl safely in her hands, she made her slow way home along the thread she had spun. The light shone before her. It shone everywhere. The people were very happy. Grandmother Spider had made this happen. Now her side of the world had light.

Even today you notice how the spider always spins her web before the sun has fully risen.

Spider Woman brought the sun to the Cherokee as well as the gift of fire. More so, she also taught the people the art of pottery.

Working with the stories

Once more Sinaa moved

FORCED MOVES

Through mime, create a small, imaginary suitcase, which will be passed round the circle. When you receive the suitcase, open it, look at the imaginary content and add something of your own. Then close the suitcase, pass it on, and so on. When everything is packed, place the imaginary suitcase in a corner of the room.

Walk around the room. Approach each other with the kind of questions we may ask our partner/child/friend before setting out on a trip, like: Have the neighbours got the keys? Did you cancel the milk? Have you got the tickets?

Return to the circle: briefly reflect on these exercises.

Paint the image evoked by the words 'Forced to move on'.

Reflect on what might have made such a forced move easier/less painful?

Share your paintings and reflections.

Tell the story 'Once more Sinaa moved'.

Paint an image of the way you feel now.

Share your paintings.

Write a 'Warning to my own people.' Include whatever you feel your own people must be warned about/against.

Share your writings.

RESPONSE TASK: as you listen to these writings select one idea which is relevant to your current life situation. Write this down.

Read through these ideas.

Select one or two which you are willing to share with the group.

Share your ideas.

Retrieve the imaginary suitcase from the place in the room where it was left. Imagine that additionally it will be packed with 'qualities needed for a difficult journey'. Each group member will pack their chosen quality. When it is fully packed, suggest that each person will have access to just such a small imaginary suitcase.

Reflect upon the entire session.

The four friends
THE RECOVERY OF JOY

Remind yourself of a place or a landscape you really like.

Describe your landscape to the others.

Select one of the images which have been shared and allow your mind to float with images of places/landscapes this evokes.

Talk a little with a partner about these associations.

Recall someone who has offered you real support during a time in your life when you truly needed it. Remind yourself of what this person is/was like.

Write something about the kind of experience this person enjoys/enjoyed or which you imagine he or she might like.

Imagine yourself in years to come. You have grown old and are reflecting on the support you were granted. Imagine too that you would like to say something about 'Giving and receiving support' to a much younger generation.

Record these thoughts and ideas.

Tell the story 'The four friends'.

Re-read what you wrote earlier about support and adjust your writings on the basis of what you have gained/learned from the story.

Share this writing with the group.

RESPONSE TASK: after having heard each statement, write one sentence which begins with 'I respect . . . '.

Talk with a partner about your 'I respect' sentences and the earlier memories.

Share some of these thoughts with the group.

Reflect upon the entire session.

Was it not an illusion?
REALISING THE DREAM

Warm up your body. Now move through the room. Imagine a central pole in the middle of the room. It is firmly fixed to the ceiling and to the floor. One by one, walk towards it. Grasp it. Use the pole to swing round it. Hug it. Move away from the imaginary pole and let it go.

Then walk through the room. Imagine that there are various ropes in the room, which you can climb. Do this simply to gain another perspective, to play, or to test your strength. Explore these imaginary ropes by yourself and with others.

Without making arrangements as to who leads and who follows, experiment with:

shadowing partner's movement;

mirroring partner's movement;
amplifying/minimalising partner's movement;
altering partner's movement.

Return to the circle.

Tell the story 'Was it not an illusion?'

Record one sentence from the story as you remember it. Think of a human situation where you can end your description/re-telling of this situation with the sentence you have chosen. Write your story.

Sequence the sentences in relation to their position in the text.

Tell the stories in this sequence.

RESPONSE TASK: create as many small pieces of paper as there are group members. When someone has completed their reading create a small gift for this person.

Distribute the gifts.

Select one which you are particularly glad to have received.

Reflect upon the entire session.

The woodcutter and the king of the mice

MUCH NEEDED REGRET

Think of words, phrases and feelings connected with regret, such as 'I'm sorry', 'Never mind', 'I promise it won't happen again'.

Take a roll of wallpaper. As if you were spray-painting graffiti, using large letters and working closely together, record as many of these statements as possible.

Having recorded these words/sentences, decorate the banner. Make sure it looks good. Take care to leave some space for later writing.

Return to the circle. Think back to a time/action which causes you regret. Maybe today; or a week ago; or much, much longer ago. Write about this occasion/omission/deed.

Share your writings.

RESPONSE TASK: as you listen to these writings, imagine that you were the one who felt such regret. Think of what might have helped you under the circumstances. Or what might help now. Write your idea/suggestion on a piece of paper, and keep it for later.

Tell the story 'The woodcutter and the king of the mice'.

Doodle: encourage group members to draw or doodle whilst listening to the story.

Distribute your remedies for a time of regret.

Read your gifts.

Select one gift which would have been particularly helpful to the woodcutter in the story and one which is particularly important for you at this stage in your life.

Take the roll of wallpaper and add your gifts to this 'Regret' banner.

Reflect on the remedies you received, upon your experiences, the story and the entire session.

How wisdom came among the tribe
RESPONSE TO CHALLENGE

Recall a dare or challenge to which you once responded.

Select one word which encapsulates the way you then felt. Record this word on a sheet of paper.

Collect these pieces of paper.

Tell the story 'How wisdom came among the tribe' up to 'It was no better than before. He could not do it.'

Select one of the words.

Write your own ending to the story. Make use of the images/solutions evoked by the word you have just chosen.

RESPONSE TASK: as you listen to the endings, ask yourself what you appreciate about this Kwaku Ananse's efforts. Write this on a small piece of paper and give it to the respective storytellers after all the story endings have been shared.

Tell the ending of 'How wisdom came among the tribe'.

Read the appreciations.

Connect the story endings with your own life experience.

Reflect upon the entire session.

Grandmother Spider brings the light
I WILL TRY

Write 'I will try . . . ' on a sheet of paper in a way which is reflective of these words. Then complete the statement.

Place these papers near one another.

RESPONSE TASK: each person takes another piece of paper and records a *sombre* response to the collection of 'I will try . . . ' statements.

Leave these responses near the 'I will try . . . ' declarations.

Reclaim your own 'I will try . . . ' paper and the sombre response closest to it.

Move to a space in the room where you can be quite separate from the other group members.

Repeat both sentences to yourself until you have a sense of the feelings they evoke for you. Notice these feelings without trying to push them away or to change them.

Return to the circle.

Tell the story 'Grandmother Spider brings the light'.

Paint five paintings which reflect your response to the story, in less than ten minutes.

Share your paintings with a partner and then with the group.

Look at the two sentences with which you have worked.

Write one sentence which contains a strong encouragement for a time of doubt.

Stand in a circle, having taken this last sentence with you.

Chant: each group member in turn will chant his/her own words of encouragement. The others echo the chant. Repeat until everyone has had their chant repeated.

Reflect upon the entire session.

A few questions to explore

o What is a tropical, rainy climate? Describe its seasons.

o What are the justifications given for the destruction of the rainforests?

o What are the main threats posed to the lives of indigenous peoples?

o How do rivers shape the land?

o What helps goats to live on poor soil? How did the soil become poor?

o What are the functions of rats? Why are they often called a pest?

o How are nets made?

o What are the threats posed to the survival of tortoises and turtles everywhere?

o What is an illusion?

o Describe the probable process of the birth of the earth and compare this with the process described in the story 'Was it not an illusion?'

o Study the form of DNA and compare this with the dream-thread.

o How do trees grow?

o When trees grow old, how old do they grow?

o What kind of community of plants and animals is supported by an average mature oak tree?

○ Why do roots matter? What is their function?

○ How are trees logged? Why does the rate and intensity of logging make all the difference to a forest? Which motives inspire intensive logging?

○ What happens to the soil and to the plant/animal/people community once a rainforest or a temperate forest disappears? What happens to the logging companies?

○ What makes palms a special group of trees?

○ How do spiders build their webs?

○ What are the rudiments of pottery making?

PART III
THE STORY FORETOLD

AND SO THEY LIVED . . .

The boughs, the sprays have stood
as motionless as stands the ancient trunk
But every leaf through all the forest flutters,
And deep the cavern of the fountain mutters.
SAMUEL TAYLOR COLERIDGE

In a moving North American Indian myth of creation the early people live in a harsh underground world. Darkness everywhere. After a long time in this great darkness they become restless. They say to each other: 'Is this all the world there is? Will there never be another world? There must be more of a world somewhere.'

As we have seen in the previous chapters these are the fundamental questions and crucial assumptions. Until the question could be formulated the early people were unable to conceive of another kind of world. How could they even have known that blue skies and howling winds existed? They lived underground, surrounded by blackness, and had never experienced light. The very thought of the possibility of a different world was therefore revolutionary. It was new. The early people's ability to think of an alternative heralded change. Once our lived reality is questioned, processes of change are set in motion. As such the pained utterance 'Will it always be like this?' is also profoundly reassuring. It signals the beginning of newness.

At the root of the quest for newness lies recognition. The early people had to feel the darkness, the lack of space, get annoyed with the way they bumped into each other. To become truly aware of the circumstances of their life. Then they had to ask the seemingly rhetorical question: 'Will it always be like this?' With the question uttered, change was unavoidable. The constrictions which the people experienced thus gave birth to the longing that somewhere, in some place, more of a world might exist. It had to exist, for the present one was too hard to bear. The story then continues.

> The early people decided to ask Mole on one of his next
> visits. Mole travelled a great deal in the underground

world and if anyone knew, Mole would. They asked:
'Mole you have wandered about. Is there more of a world
than this? Is there more of a world somewhere?'

Mole replied: 'Indeed, I do travel here and there. I
know the dark world which surrounds us. From time to
time, when I dig my way upwards, the world feels
different. It seems different. My eyes cannot see and
therefore I cannot tell you. Maybe you can travel with me
and find out yourselves. Maybe this is all the world there
is or maybe there is more of a world up there.'

After Mole had promised to tell the early people when
he sensed the new world, the people made ready to follow
him. He dug his way upwards. He clawed and he clawed.
The earth was passed down the line from one person to
the next. The tunnel which Mole dug towards the new
world was thus closed behind the early people. They
could never find their way back. The tunnel to the old
world was forever closed.

Mole told them when he sensed the different air. He
need not have spoken. The light was everywhere and it
hurt the early people's eyes. It hurt them sorely. They
covered their eyes with their hands and one of them said:
'This is not good. It is as bad as the darkness. Here we can
see nothing either. Let us go back.'

They argued bitterly.

At this stage of their story-journey we shall leave the Tewa myth. We

can see the early people sitting or standing with their hands and paws in front of their eyes. There is too much light and it hurts. They regret their decision and want to return to the old ways. But the road back has been forever closed, whilst the road forwards cannot yet be seen. They dare not, cannot look. In the new world familiar habits lost their efficacy. Adjustments were necessary, but where to find the energy for such adjustments, given that the first part of the journey had already demanded a great deal! Having arrived at their first resting place the early people were exposed to the impact of all that had been lost: the old dwelling place, the predictable ways of bumping into one another, the constrained space which had been home. Their dissatisfaction had fuelled the desire for change. However, they had not bargained for the cost of pain once they arrived in their new environment. The people's calculation had merely included satisfactions resulting from the absence of constraints. Pleasure had been anticipated as the reward for the willingness to take risks. Not suffering. Thus they were unprepared for the fear, confusion and regrets which are such predictable components of the journey towards a different world.

When beginning a process of change, we regularly start from a place of depletion, hardly aware that when we are out of tune with ourselves, our dreams become all the more important. They keep us going. Our diminishing energy is temporarily rekindled by the hope of an early harvest. A harvest which, however, rarely arrives at the time when we expect and need it. For when we reach the new home, the different job, the new partner, we soon discover that the rewards are as implicit as the seed which lies hidden in the winter soil. While now we remember even more poignantly the fading colours of autumn. We call this 'disillusionment'.

The Tewa Indians knew that the journey toward newness involves the disillusionment of the dreams which are of our own making. Erich Fromm says: 'Genuine love is an expression of productiveness and implies care, respect, responsibility and knowledge. It is not an effect in the sense of being affected by somebody, but an active striving for the growth and happiness of the loved person, rooted in one's own capacity to love.' If Mole had been able to see, he could have warned the early people about the risk of arrival in newness. But he could not see. However, when we participate in a group we are able to share some of our knowledge of the processes of change with each other, so that when the going gets tough – as it invariably does – we are safeguarded by a shared understanding of the appearance of such storms and prepared to cope with the resultant sense of disorientation. In other words, the group learns through anticipation how to adjust to newness.

Once we are truly aware of the threats posed to our beloved planet and to the survival of so many species which are at home on earth, we are probably terrified. We can only move beyond such fears if we accept that we must get to know them fully, so that we may see more clearly the resistance to bringing about protective change. Especially when we feel crippled by the seeming inertness of mega-corporations and transnational organisations, we must create breathing spaces during which we can collect ourselves sufficiently to stop being tossed about here and there. To cease from responding merely to the immediacy of situations.

During times of crisis, and this is one, we desperately need reflection and clarity of vision. To act with presence of mind. Let us therefore encourage one another to keep still long enough and in sufficiently lovely ways. Return to our own still centre. To be re-inspired. To rekindle our love.

Whenever stories are told, stillness falls. We cease our restless frittering. During these times of concentrated devotion to alternative realms we may reconnect with the power of creation. We rest momentarily. Through such resting we are renewed. Renewal inspires the courage to change.

TO TAKE YOU FURTHER

A selection of myths and folktales

Baumann, H., (1972) *Hero Legends of the World*, Dent & Sons.
Benedict, R., (1931) *Tales of the Chociti Indians*, USGPO.
Berg, L., (1977) *Folk Tales*, Pan Books.
Bierhorst, J. (ed), (1976) *The Red Swan*, McGraw Hill.
Briggs, K.M., (1977) *British Folktales*, Ayer.
Calvino, I., (1981) *Italian Folktales*, Pantheon.
Cameron, A., (1984) *Daughters of Copperwoman*, Women's Press.
Chandler, D., (1978) *Favourite Stories from Cambodia*, Heinemann.
Crown, A.C., (1971) *Tales from Poland*, Pergamon Press.
Darwood, N.Y., (1973) *Tales from the Thousand and One Nights*, Penguin.
Erdoes, R. and Ortiz, A., (1984) *American Indian Myths and Legends*, Pantheon.
Feldmann, S. (ed) (1975) *African Myths & Tales*, Dell.
Garner, A., (1980) *The Guizer*, Fontana Lions.
Graves, R., (1982) *Greek Myths*, Doubleday.
Green, L., (1979) *Tales from Hispanic Lands*, Silver.
Grimm, Jacob, *Grimm's Fairytales*, Puffin.
Hall, E.S., Jr., (1975) *The Eskimo Storyteller*, University of Tennessee Press.
Hooke, S.H., (1963) *Middle Eastern Mythology*, Penguin.
Jacobs, J., (1968) *Celtic Fairy Tales*, Dover.
Knappert, J., (1970) *Myths and Legends of the Swahili*, Heinemann.
Langloh Parker, K., (1934) *Australian Legendary Tales*.
Lee, F.H., (1931) *Folktales of All Nations*, Harrap.
Manning-Sanders, R., (1979) *Fox Tales*, Magnet.
Marriott, A. & Rachin, C.K., (1968) *American Indian Mythology*, Mentor Books.
Marriott, A. & Rachin, C.K., (1975) *Plains Indian Mythology*, Mentor Books.
Mountford, C.P., (1976) *Before Time Began*, Nelson.
Parrinder, G., (1967) *African Mythology*, Hamlyn.
Piggott, J., (1969) *Japanese Mythology*, Hamlyn.
Radin, P. & Sweeney, J., (1952) *African Folktales and Sculpture*, Bollingen Foundation.
Ransome, A., (1916) *Old Peter's Russian Tales*, Nelson.
Reed, A.W., (1984) *Aboriginal Myths, Tales of the Dreamtime*, Reed Books.
Roberts, R., (1979) *Chinese Fairy Tales and Fantasies*, Pantheon Books.
Sharma, N., (1971) *Folktales of Nepal*, Sterlin Publishers.

Siek, M., (1972) *Favourite Stories from Indonesia*, Heinemann Educational Books (Asia) Ltd.
Thompson, S., (1966) *Tales of the North American Indians*, Indiana University Press.
Timpanelli, G., (1984) *Tales from the Roof of the World*, Viking.
Todd, L., (1985) *Tortoise, the Trickster*, Routledge and Kegan Paul.
VanOver, R., (1980) *Sunsongs*, Mentor Books.
Williamson, D., (1985) *The Broonies Silkies and Fairies*, Canongate.
Wolkstein, D., (1980) *The Magic Orange Tree & Other Haitian Folktales*, Schocken.

The Oxford Myths and Legends series and the Pantheon Fairy Tale and Folklore Library also offer fine sources of myths and folktales.

Books about myths, folktales and storytelling

Bettelheim, B., (1978) *The Uses of Enchantment*, Penguin.
Campbell, J., (1988) *The Power of Myth*, Doubleday.
Colwell, E., (1990) *Storytelling*, Thimble Press.
Dieckmann, H., (1986) *Twice Told Tales*, Chiron.
Dunne, J.S., (1973) *Time and Myth*, SCM Press.
Gersie, A., (1991) *Storymaking in Bereavement*, Jessica Kingsley.
Gersie, A. and King, N., (1990) *Storymaking in Education and Therapy*, Jessica Kingsley.
Propp, V., (1984) *Morphology of the Folktale*, University of Texas Press.
Sawyer, R., (1986) *The Way of the Storyteller*, Penguin.
Thompson, S., (1977) *The Folktale*, University of California Press.
Travers, A.P., (1980) *What the Bee Knows*, Aquarian Press.
Wells, G., (1987) *The Meaning Makers*, Hodder & Stoughton.
Wootton, A., (1986) *Animal Folklore, Myth and Legend*, Blandford Press.
Zipes, J., (1983) *The Trials and Tribulations of Little Red Riding Hood*, Bergin and Garvey.

Organisations which can be contacted for further information regarding storytellers, storytelling training and other events

For a list of British storytellers, contact: **The Children's Book Foundation**, Book House, 45 East Hill, London SW18 2QZ. Enquire as to cost.

Adult Literacy and Basic Skills Unit, Kingsbourne House, 229-231 High Holborn, London WC1 7DA.

English Folk Dance and Song Society, Cecil Sharp House, 2 Regents Park Road, London NW1.

National Oracy Project, Newcombe House, 45 Notting Hill Gate, London W11 3JB.

Storybox, Department of Teaching Studies, Bradford and Ilkley Community College, Trinity Road, Bradford BD7 1AY.

The College of Storytellers, Freepost, London NW3 1YB.

Yarn Spinning, Linen Hall Library, Belfast.

Age Exchange Reminiscence Centre, 15 Camden Road, Blackheath, London SE3 0QA.

In the United States:

Writing and Storytelling: an annual Festival at the University of Nebraska, Division of Continuing Studies, Lincoln, Nebraska.

National Association for the Preservation and Perpetuation of Storytelling, PO Box 309, Jonesborough, TN 37659.

Order of Ears, 12019 Donohue Avenne, Lonisville, Kentucky 40243.

Jewish Storytelling Center, 92nd Street YM-YWHA Library, 1395 Lexington Avenue, New York, NY 10128.

Lesley College (Storytelling Center), 29 Everett Street, Cambridge, Massachusetts.

In Australia:

Brown's Mart Community Arts Project, Smith Street, PO Box 2429, Darwin, NT 5794.

Community Arts Network, 77 Salamanca Place, Hobart, TAS 7000.

Network, 66 Albion Street, Surry Hills, NSW 2010.

Out-Reach, Foleys Road, PO Box 1223, North Wollongong, NSW 2500.

In New Zealand:

Theatre Corporate, 14 Galatos Street, Auckland 1.

In South Africa:

Drama Outreach Project, 4 Virginia Avenue, Vredehoek, Cape Town 8001.

INDEX